P9-DNF-937

CHICAGO CUBS

WHERE HAVE YOU GONE?

CHICAGO CUBS
WHERE HAVE YOU GONE?

ERNIE BANKS, ANDY PAFKO, FERGUSON JENKINS, AND OTHER CUBS GREATS

FRED MITCHELL

FOREWORD BY **STEVE STONE**

SPORTS
PUBLISHING

Sports Publishing books may be purchased in bulk at special discounts for
sales promotion, corporate gifts, fund-raising, or educational purposes.
Special editions can also be created to specifications. For details, contact
the Special Sales Department, Sports Publishing, 307 West 36th Street,
11th Floor, New York, NY 10018 or sportspub-
books@skyhorsepublishing.com.

Sports Publishing® is a registered trademark of Skyhorse Publishing, Inc.®,
a Delaware corporation.

Visit our website at www.sportspubbooks.com.

10 9 8 7 6 5 4 3 2 1

Library of Congress Cataloging-in-Publication Data is available on file.

ISBN: 978-1-61321-201-1

Printed in the United States of America

To Kim,
my awesome, compassionate wife,
companion and sports enthusiast.

And to our little slugger, Cameron,
already a Hall of Famer in my eyes.

CONTENTS

Foreword viii
Acknowledgments ix
Introduction x

ERNIE BANKS 2
ROD BECK 8
GLENN BECKERT 14
LARRY BOWA .20
BILL BUCKNER 28
JOSE CARDENAL 34
RON CEY 40
JODY DAVIS 46
ANDRE DAWSON 52
BOBBY DERNIER 58
SHAWON DUNSTON 64
LEON DURHAM 70
DENNIS ECKERSLEY 76
LEE ELIA 82
MARK GRACE .88
RICHIE HEBNER 94
KEN HOLTZMAN 100
BURT HOOTON 106
RANDY HUNDLEY 112
DARRIN JACKSON 120
FERGUSON JENKINS 126
DON KESSINGER 132

DAVE KINGMAN .... .138
PETE LACOCK .... .144
VANCE LAW .... .150
ED LYNCH .... .158
KEITH MORELAND .... .164
DICKIE NOLES .... .170
ANDY PAFKO .... .178
MILT PAPPAS .... .184
RYNE SANDBERG .... .190
SCOTT SANDERSON .... .194
RON SANTO .... .198
LEE SMITH .... .204
TIM STODDARD .... .212
STEVE STONE .... .220
RICK SUTCLIFFE .... .226
STEVE TROUT .... .232
BILLY WILLIAMS .... .238
KERRY WOOD .... .246
DON ZIMMER .... .252

FOREWORD

I wrote a book a few years back called *Where is Harry?* It turns out that was the No. 1 question I always got from Cubs fans over the many years I worked with broadcast legend Harry Caray in the booth.

That observation really let me know that Cubs fans are loyal and that they also have an obsession to know where Cubs players of old are. And that is what led sportswriter Fred Mitchell to profile 40 former Cubs in this inspiring compilation of *Cubs: Where Have You Gone?* This book will satisfy and fascinate every baseball fan.

Although I enjoyed my greatest success in baseball as a pitcher with the Baltimore Orioles, I truly enjoyed my brief stint with the Cubs. I especially remember 1975. We had a division lead into June and *Sports Illustrated* did a story on us. It was astonishing to me, looking at the makeup of that team, that we would have the lead. Eventually, the real contenders contended and the pretenders pretended. But what I will remember most about that season was that there was a very small yet extremely loyal Cubs following.

That loyal following would multiply over the years. I remember that there was always a special feeling about the ballpark. There is something about Wrigley Field. That is the one link that Cubs fans will always have.

The convergence of the Tribune Company buying the franchise in the early '80s, WGN television becoming a satellite station and the arrival of legendary broadcaster Harry Caray led to the immense popularity of the Chicago Cubs, who would draw three million fans in 2004.

Credit should go to Cubs president Andy MacPhail for realizing the overall potential of this franchise.

So sit back and enjoy *Cubs: Where Have You Gone?* Savor the memories.

—STEVE STONE

ACKNOWLEDGMENTS

Thanks to the *Chicago Tribune* and assistant managing editor/sports Dan McGrath, sports editor Bill Adee and assistant sports editor Ken Paxson; to Sports Publishing L.L.C. developmental editor David Brauer; the Chicago Cubs: media relations director Sharon Pannozzo and community relations representative Rebecca Polihronis; and former Cubs vice president Ned Colletti and former Cubs media relations director Bob Ibach.

INTRODUCTION

In a franchise that has celebrated near misses as if they were true championships, the Chicago Cubs' global family seems to revel in the role of the underdog.

The late Hall of Fame Chicago sportscaster Jack Brickhouse often said that "any team can have a bad century," noting that the Cubs had not won a World Series title since 1908. But encouraging developments in recent years suggest the wait may not last much longer.

In fact, the 2004 Cubs of manager Dusty Baker were installed as preseason favorites to advance to the Fall Classic after last year's—you got it—near miss.

That may have been an ambitious prediction, considering the fact the Cubs had not put together back-to-back winning seasons since 1971-72.

Fittingly, this is the 29th anniversary of the 1984 Cubs' divisional title. That team came within three innings of dispatching the San Diego Padres in the National League Championship Series at Jack Murphy Stadium and facing the Detroit Tigers in the World Series.

As the beat writer for the *Chicago Tribune* covering the Cubs that season, I can remember it as if it were, well, 20 years ago.

Those 1984 Cubs ended 39 years of frustration by clinching the National League East title in Pittsburgh. A cozy crowd of only 5,472—perhaps half from Chicago—was on hand for that historic event at Three Rivers Stadium.

With one out to go on that memorable evening, Cubs general manager Dallas Green leaned over and kissed his wife, Sylvia.

On the field, Leon "Bull" Durham held up two fingers and bellowed, "One more out to go."

The laid-back Ryne Sandberg glanced across the infield at Larry Bowa and allowed an ear-to-ear smile.

"Is this it?" Sandberg asked sheepishly.

"Yeah, Ryno. This is it, brother," Bowa replied.

A moment later—the magic moment—the Cubs' magic number wound down to zero. Rick Sutcliffe caught the corner on the Pirates' Joe Orsulak for a called third strike.

The Cubs would go on to win division titles in 1989 and 2003 with a wild card spot thrown in in 1998, only to be denied field and clubhouse access to the World Series. The last time the Cubs played in a World Series was 1945, when they lost to the Detroit Tigers. Are you old enough to remember that season?

But Cubs fans know all of those gory details already. Despite the unfathomable Cubs collapse of 1969, they would rather dwell on the feats of Hall of Fame players Ernie Banks, Billy Williams and Ferguson Jenkins, as well as perennial All-Stars such as Ron Santo, Andre Dawson, Mark Grace and Sandberg.

Wrigley Field was booked solid for a celebration every time the Cubs hosted a game in 2004, establishing an all-time attendance record. Celebrities flock to the Cubs' shrine as if it were a holy sanctuary. Actors Bill Murray, John Cusack, Nicolas Cage, Gary Sinise, Jeff Garlin and comedian Tom Dressen seem to enjoy spending more time at the ballpark on the corner of Clark and Addison than they do in Hollywood.

Murray even named one of his sons "Homer Banks Murray" in honor of his childhood idol, "Mr. Cub" Ernie Banks.

Former Cubs players, entertainers, and politicians reinforce the memory of the legendary broadcaster Harry Caray by singing "Take Me Out to the Ballgame" during the seventh inning of every Cubs home game.

The atmosphere is much more festive than it must have been in 1908, when the Cubs played their home games at the old West Side Grounds, located at Polk and Lincoln (now Wolcott) streets in Chicago.

Baseball record books tell us that Mordecai "Three Finger" Brown won 29 games in 1908 for the Cubs. And the double play combination of Joe Tinker, Johnny Evers and Frank Chance was lyrical, if not unbeatable.

This book helps us catch up with the life and times of 41 former Cubs, spanning seven decades.

If the Cubs ever do win another World Series, it will be the arduous journey to that nirvana that will be remembered at least as much as actually reaching the elusive goal. No doubt, Cubs fans will be shouting from the Wrigleyville rooftops.

—FRED MITCHELL

NOTE TO READERS: Though I have gone through and updated a lot of the information that was outdated from the first publication of *Cubs Where Have You Gone?* in 2004, much of the existing text and quotes remain.

CHICAGO CUBS
WHERE HAVE YOU GONE?

ERNIE BANKS

He will forever be known as Mr. Cub, a prolific-hitting infielder whose radiant disposition has branded him one of baseball's finest ambassadors.

The National League Most Valuable Player in 1958 and 1959 while playing shortstop, Banks was switched to first base in mid-career.

A first-ballot Hall of Famer, Banks played his entire career with the Cubs (1953-1971). He was a 11-time All-Star and won a Gold Glove at shortstop in 1960.

His best season was 1959 when he led the National League in RBI with 143 and belted 43 home runs. Defensively, he led all shortstops with a .985 fielding average. Banks batted .304 with a .596 slugging percentage and 97 runs scored. He is considered one of the greatest players in the history of the game never to make it to the postseason.

Banks played shortstop from 1953-1961. From 1962-1971, he was a first baseman, where he showed excellent range and a strong arm. In fact, Banks played more games at first base (1,259) than shortstop (1,125), but he is remembered more as a shortstop.

In 1955, Banks hit a record five grand slams, the last one off rookie Lindy McDaniel on September 19. The five grand slams broke the record of four previously shared by Babe Ruth, Lou Gehrig, Ralph Kiner,

Brace Photo

14 · ERNIE BANKS · SS
Years with the Cubs: 1953-71

Two-time NL MVP (1958-59) • 11-time All-Star • 1960 NL Gold Glove Award • Hit 47 HR in 1958 and had 143 RBI in 1959 • Topped 40 HR in five seasons and had 100 RBI in eight seasons • Hit 512 career HR and had 1,636 career RBI • Elected to Baseball Hall of Fame in 1977

Frank Schulte, Rudy York, Tommy Henrich, Vince DiMaggio, Sid Gordon, Al Rosen and Ray Boone.

Banks also broke Vern Stephens's record for most home runs by a shortstop in a single season. From 1955 to 1960, Banks's 248 home runs were more than anyone else in the majors, including Mickey Mantle, Willie Mays, and Henry Aaron.

Banks, who turned 81 on January 31, 2012, remains vibrant and optimistic about his life and the future of his beloved Cubs.

"I have a lot of goals. I guess I have always been that way in my life," said Banks in 2004.

"First of all I want to achieve my master's in finance from Northwestern," he said in 2004. "I want to build an image as a business person. I want to keep sports a part of my life, as always. I want to write two books. One would be called *Live Above and Beyond.* Because that is what I think of my life. I want to be around people who live above and beyond and write a book about them. It doesn't have to be something done in sports. It could be a woman who raises five kids by herself.

"My last, but not least, goal is to become the first former professional athlete to win the Nobel Peace Prize. I used to dream about this 30 years ago. I am not trying to drop names, but I called up a friend of mine—actor Sydney Poitier. I said: 'Sydney, I want to win the Nobel Peace Prize. How do I get there?'

"He said: 'Well, Ernie, you have no chance.' And we laughed. He said, 'First, you have to be international. You have to be known in America and some other country for doing something worthwhile. And you haven't done that yet.' I said: 'Well, I still have a little time.'"

Banks's all-time Cubs career home run record of 512 was broken by Sammy Sosa in May of 2004.

"I just knew it was coming," said Banks. "There is no finer person that I would have liked to have seen break it other than Sammy. He is a tremendous player and a wonderful human being. I could see Sammy's ability when he first came to the Cubs, and then he hit over 60 home runs three years in a row. His rhythm and timing and attitude are all there."

In addition to his Hall of Fame numbers and records on the field, Banks takes tremendous pride in being known as "Mr. Cub."

"That's kind of what my life has always been about. I wanted to finish my career with one team, in one city, one mayor, one park, one owner. I did that. When I first started, Mayor [Richard J.] Daley was the mayor. The Wrigleys owned the team. We played all of our home games at Wrigley Field during the daytime. So my career was very unique and

I am proud of it. I have been involved in the city of Chicago and with Little Leagues all around the city and suburbs. It was a fun and enjoyable time both on the field and off the field. Now I meet a lot of people who used to come out to Wrigley Field when they were kids and they are older now. They still remember those days," he said.

Banks has even taken the time to talk to Sosa about his responsibilities as a baseball icon.

"Two years ago Sammy invited me down to his home in the Dominican," said Banks in 2004. "I played golf with him almost every day there. It was just fun being around him and to talk to him about playing and his ideas and goals. He said, 'In eight years I am going to be in the Hall of Fame!' I said: 'Yeah, yeah, you are.' He is just a cordial, smart young man. He's like my son. I wish I had learned Spanish when I was younger so I could communicate with him a little bit more. But he understands English very well. And he has great people skills. I am sure Sammy understands that Wrigley Field is the perfect place to play baseball. He has a lot of flair when he hits a home run and gets all excited when he jumps up. He has a unique style. He is out there to satisfy people."

Legendary sportscaster Harry Caray broadcast a baseball game in 1953 for radio station KMOX in St. Louis between the Cardinals and the Cubs, in which Banks, then a Cubs rookie, hit the first of his 512 career home runs.

And Caray became a hit in Banks's eyes thereafter.

"I hit it off of Jerry Staley," Banks recalled. "The next night before the game, Harry came down around the batting cage. He came up to me and introduced himself. I was still just a kid and I was very shy. Harry said with great enthusiasm, 'Ernie Banks! Boy, you hit a tremendous pitch out of the ballpark last night. You are going to be a great hitter.'

"I said, 'Well, thank you you very much.'

"Harry was very complimentary. He told me I had quick wrists and he wished me well. I thought that was very nice. I didn't have any idea about broadcasters and announcers then because I had come from the Kansas City Monarchs [of the old Negro League], and we had no announcers or broadcasts then.

"My old teammate and mentor with the Cubs, second baseman Gene Baker, later told me that Harry Caray was the top broadcaster for the Cardinals. Gene said, 'Do you know that KMOX has a range of 500 miles as a station?'

"I said, 'You mean they can hear it in Dallas [Banks's hometown], too?'

"Gene said, 'I don't know about Dallas, but a lot of people can hear the games.'

"I was so naive, but Harry and Gene both kind of settled me down. And I quickly learned about the power Harry had on the air as a broadcaster."

Banks has been credited over the years as a tremendous ambassador for the game of baseball in his own inimitable way; and, of course, Caray was a walking billboard for the game on the airwaves.

"Harry was even greater," said Banks. "Watching Harry when he came around the batting cage, and the interest all of the players had in him, and the interest the fans had in him showed me he was a very powerful man in baseball. Kids and seniors and men and women...his saying 'Holy Cow!' was symbolic in the game of baseball.

"His technique and style and personality added a unique flavor to the game."

Banks spent his entire major league career with the Cubs. And Caray spent 53 years broadcasting major league baseball.

"It is remarkable," said Banks. "It shows a lot of love and it shows compassion for people. And it shows his intelligence for the game. Harry went through the Jackie Robinson period. When Jackie came up to the majors in 1947, folks tell me that black people could not sit in the main section of the ballpark grandstand in St. Louis's old Busch Stadium. When Jackie and the Dodgers came to St. Louis, it was always a sellout and a lot of blacks came to the game. Harry went through that period of change in baseball. To me, that was the biggest change and most powerful change in all of sports.

"Harry also had a chance to see Larry Doby for a little while when he managed the White Sox. So Harry saw a broad spectrum of social change that most of us never realized. He saw a lot.

"With all of the changes in the game—from expansion to free agency, to the orange baseball and Charlie Finley, all of the labor strikes, and all of that—Harry went through all of that with a very positive outlook on the game. Harry gave his views, but his views were always very positive. What he said was from the heart."

Banks's popularity spans many decades.

In fact, renowned film star and comedian Bill Murray, a Chicago native and lifelong Cubs fan, named his son "Homer Banks Murray" in honor of his idol.

The Cubs organization paid Banks the ultimate compliment when a statue of his likeness was erected and unveiled just outside Wrigley Field near the corner of Clark and Addison Streets at the start of the 2008 season.

"When I am not here, this will be here," Banks joked as he pointed to the sculpture.

On hand for the ceremony were many distinguished civic leaders and politicians, as well as former teammates. Hall of Famer Henry Aaron, a longtime friend of Banks, also was in attendance. Banks appeared moved by the special honor.

"This should have happened 10 or 15 years ago," said Aaron, who added that Banks was "the greatest ambassador for baseball, and still is a great ambassador for baseball."

The statue, by suburban Chicago sculptor Lou Cella, depicts "Mr. Cub" at bat with his signature stance.

Billy Williams offered a tribute to Banks, as did Ron Santo. Ferguson Jenkins also attended the event emceed by Cubs executive Crane Kenney in a drizzle.

"Is that me?" Banks repeated as he glanced at the statue and addressed various dignitaries.

Banks later addressed the crowd and talked about his parents, who raised him in Dallas. His father had just a 3rd-grade education and his mother a 6th-grade education.

"But they were very wise," he said.

Banks referred to the statue as "a miracle" as dozens of fans who lined the sidewalk began to chant "Er-nie! Er-nie!"

Where Have You Gone?

ROD BECK

Rod Beck, who many knew as "Shooter," recorded 58 saves for the Cubs in their 1998 playoff season. On June 23, 2007, Beck was found dead in Phoenix, Ariz. Cocaine was found in his home and bedroom. He was just 38.

Throughout his baseball career, Beck was a man of the people, always eager to take time to chat with fans, and for several months in 2003, Beck lived in a van down by the river.

"It's really a pretty cool place; I'm not trailer trash," Beck said with broad a smile before offering a cold brew as he guided a visitor through his state-of-the-art 36-foot Winnebago Journey DL.

The three-time former All-Star reliever was rehabbing his surgically repaired right arm by pitching for the Triple A Iowa Cubs. He lived in his RV, which was parked just behind the center field scoreboard of Sec Taylor Stadium and about 50 yards from the Des Moines River.

Following a game against the Omaha Royals, fans Ryan Putnam, Bryan Putnam and Sean Dumm of Kansas City blew off a wedding reception to stop by Beck's motor home.

"The reception wasn't very exciting," said Dumm. "We heard that 'The Shooter' was in town, so we decided to stop by to meet him."

David Seelig/Getty Images

47 · ROD BECK · P
Years with Cubs: 1998-99

51 Saves in 1998 (2nd in NL) • Led NL with 81 appearances and 70 games finished in 1998 • Pitched in 1998 NLDS • Totaled 112 appearances and 58 saves with Cubs

Greeting fans inside and outside his van after games became customary for Beck, who considers himself "a blue-collar guy" at heart.

"Fans say, 'We'll meet you out at your motor home after the game.' I say, 'Oh, all right, whatever. It actually was fun," said Beck.

"The people in Des Moines are nice people. At first I was thinking: 'I hope I don't pitch bad, because then they will put spray paint on it.' But I am originally from Los Angeles. That's what happens in L.A. The people out here have been great. A fireman stopped by the other night. A state policeman stopped by. At first I thought I was in trouble. But they would just come by and ask for an autograph and hang out. And I have had some people come by when they were not on duty and have a beer or whatever. It has been quite the adventure."

With a shaved head and fu manchu, Beck remained unpretentious.

"I am just regular people like anyone else. I just happen to be on television," he said. "If plumbing was a sport and they were on TV, they would be heroes and sign autographs. Ballplayers would be blue-collar. I take the same approach. I am a blue-collar guy and do my job. If people think it's exciting, I am flattered by it. If they want [an autograph], that's cool. I don't know what they are going to do with it."

Beck missed the entire 2002 season to have "Tommy John" surgery on his right elbow. After two seasons with the Boston Red Sox, he signed a minor league contract with the Cubs—a team he helped send to the 1998 NL playoffs with 51 saves.

"The best fun I ever had was with the '98 Cubs," said Beck. "That's because there has been so much futility with the Cubs. To win the wild card and make the playoffs...the way the city treated us was great. It was the first year after [Hall of Fame broadcaster] Harry Caray had passed. Then we had that eerie night of the 163rd game when we had to play the Giants. Then to beat the team that ultimately was still paying me was funny. So they paid me to beat them that night. Dusty [Baker] was in the other dugout and the Harry Caray balloon was floating in the air. It was eerie."

With 266 career saves in the majors at the time, Beck was eager to be called up by the big club. He performed well in spring training for the Cubs (2.16 ERA in eight and one-third innings), but his fastball that timed out at 98 miles an hour for the Giants a decade ago had lost about 20 miles of zip following the surgery.

"I thought I was only going to be down here [in Des Moines] two weeks, or three weeks maybe," said Beck. "So I figured, rather than coming down here and getting an apartment with some furniture and paying the phone bill, I said I will just take my own stuff. I called the people here and asked them about bringing the RV. They said 'Sure, we'll find somewhere for you to put it.'"

Beck had started driving from his home in Scottsdale, Arizona, earlier last spring and only got as far as Amarillo, Texas, over a period of three days.

"I dropped a line fishing here and there," Beck explained. He then summoned his brother to help him drive the rest of the way to Des Moines.

"My family [wife Stacey and two daughters] came up here for a week and lived in here with me. It's like going camping and playing baseball at the same time. What's better than that?"

Beck was a popular addition to his teammates with the Iowa Cubs.

"Shooter is as good as they come," said former Iowa Cubs second baseman Bobby Hill. "The guy is never bitter, always smiling and always laughing. Everyone goes to his place every once in a while. He makes it fun down here. To see a guy with so much time in the big leagues and still have fun is good to see."

Former Los Angeles Dodgers pitcher Jerry Reuss was encouraged by Beck's progress.

"I think as time goes by, his prospects are better," said Reuss. "Could he go up there now and do well? Sure he could. But I hedge the bet. The way I see it [the Cubs] are going to give him some time to get as strong as he can. If a need develops up there, I am sure he will be someone who fits in their plans. He has the [guts] of a cat burglar. I give him credit for having all the heart in the world."

Beck was not hedging his bets.

"I'm ready, as far as I am concerned," said Beck. "While I am here I am probably going to gain more miles per hour on my fastball and have more consistency. Every once in a while I will hit 89 miles an hour, then I might average 84 the next day and 86 the next. So I know the possibility for increasing the speed is still there. But I know that what I have right now is more than good enough. I am confident in my ability."

Beck, who struck out five batters in one and one-third innings of work on May 9, 2003, asserted that speed isn't everything when it comes to getting big-league batters out.

"It depends on the person," he said. "Granted, if you throw in the mid-90s, you can get away with more mistakes. If you put the ball where you want to and you know how to pitch and you've got [guts], you can get away with less. That's the category where I come under. I know how to pitch and I can put it where I want to nine times out of 10, and I am going to find a way to get it done. For me, I am ready. Then again, I thought I was ready in the spring. But topping out at 78 [miles an hour] and topping out at 89 are a little bit different. So I understood the reasoning behind sending me down. I also know that now I am ready."

Beck was given permission to talk to other major league clubs, although rejoining the Cubs was his first choice.

"Eight teams called and three teams offered big-league jobs. I have turned them down because I want to play for the Cubs," he said. "It has kind of been a strange situation. I don't need the major league time [for his pension] and I don't need the money. But I am 34 saves shy of 300; I would like to do that. I am 34 years old. What am I going to do? Sit around and go fishing the rest of my life? I have all kind of time to do that. I did all the work during rehab. My daughters had a good time when I was there. They said' 'Daddy, we want to see you pitch.' I have to go pitch. They are at home, so I have to be on TV. We are not on TV down here [in Des Moines]. We have to find somewhere that it is."

If the Cubs had called him up, Beck wasn't planning to bring the van to Chicago.

"I don't think there are too many places in Chicago to park that thing," said Beck. "Going on road trips and leaving that RV in the Wrigley Field parking lot wouldn't be good."

When the Cubs finally decided to take a pass on bringing Beck back to the big club, he signed with the San Diego Padres in the fall of 2003. Beck left the Padres for "personal reasons" during spring training of 2004 and later returned to their ball club.His final major league appearance was August 14, 2004. He finished with 286 career saves in 13 seasons.

Where Have You Gone?

GLENN BECKERT

A four-time All-Star second baseman for the Cubs from 1965 to 1973, Glenn Beckert can sympathize with many Cubs fans.

After watching the 2003 Cubs team come within five outs of advancing to the World Series, most Cubs fans figured their team would win it all in 2004. Beckert recalled similar optimism after the Cubs came so close to making it to the World Series in 1969.

"It is so much harder being a fan than being a player," said Beckert, who hit .291 with 22 doubles in 1969. "If you are a player and you have a bad day, you say, 'OK, we'll get 'em tomorrow.' But when you are a fan, all you can do is watch TV and wonder, 'How did he miss that play?'"

"I can't believe that in the city of Chicago we are still remembered, even though we didn't make the playoffs," Beckert said. "The '69 Mets reminded me a lot of the Florida Marlins [in 2003]. People were saying' 'Who are these guys?' They weren't recognized, there were no big names on their team. It was the same way with the Marlins. Now these kids will become stars."

Beckert, who finished his big-league career in San Diego in 1974 and '75, was a .283 career hitter. But his enduring memories are with his former Cubs teammates.

Brace Photo

18 · GLENN BECKERT · 2B
Years with Cubs: 1965-73

Four-time All-Star • 1968 NL Gold Glove Award • Led NL with 98 runs scored in 1968 • Totaled 672 runs scored and 353 RBI with Cubs

"We were very fortunate that the nucleus of our team was able to play together for nine years. That is not done too much any more," said Beckert.

The 1969 season was bittersweet for the Cubs. Or perhaps a better way to put it for Cubs fans is sweet-bitter.

"Right after the 1969 season, [teammate and friend] Ronnie [Santo] said to me, 'Let's get away from baseball. Let's go to Las Vegas.' So we go to one of the big casinos there. We started playing blackjack and we said to each other: 'Isn't this great? We don't have to listen to the World Series and all that stuff.' Then they opened up a 100-foot screen right in front of us showing the Mets and Orioles playing in the World Series. Ronnie said, 'Let's get the heck out of here.'"

Santo, who passed away in 2010, suffered from diabetes but kept his ailment to himself during his playing days.

"I remember when I was a rookie and I was hitting .205 or something and Ronnie was hitting .335," said Beckert of his days of traveling with Santo.

"We were rooming together and I saw him in the bathroom giving himself an injection. I didn't know what he was doing. I didn't know anything about insulin injections or diabetes. So I said, 'No wonder you're hitting .335. Give me a shot of that stuff.' Then he explained to me that he was a diabetic and had to take his insulin shot every morning."

Born October 12, 1940, in Pittsburgh, Pennsylvania, Glenn Alfred Beckert was originally signed by Boston as an amateur free agent in 1962. He made his major league debut on April 12, 1965 with the Cubs, where he hit .239 in his rookie season. Beckert had been selected from the Red Sox in November of 1962 in what was then called the first-year players draft.

At the end of his Cubs career, he was traded to San Diego along with Bobby Fenwick on November 7, 1973, in exchange for outfielder Jerry Morales.

The Padres released Beckert April 28, 1975.

In 1969, 24 years after their previous postseason appearance, the Cubs seemed primed to end their playoff drought. On August 13, 1969, with a little more than a month and a half to go in the regular season, the Cubs enjoyed a nine and a half-game lead over the New York Mets. Just two weeks later, the lead was reduced to two games. The Cubs then lost eight in a row in September while the Mets won 10 in a row. The Cubs finished eight games out of first place, and they missed the postseason again following one of the worst collapses in baseball history.

Entering the 2004 season, the Cubs hadn't been to the World Series since 1945. They failed to make the playoffs between 1945 and 1984, a period of 39 years. The Cubs did manage to earn playoff berths in 1984, 1989, and 1998 and 2003, when they won a playoff round (against Atlanta) for the first time in over 50 years.

But the 1969 season seemed to give birth to the notion that the Cubs were the lovable losers.

In the opener at Wrigley Field in '69, the Cubs fell behind the Phillies 6-5 and had one man on base in the 11th inning when Willie Smith stepped to the plate. Smith hit a pinch home run into the right field bleachers to give the Cubs the victory. The Cubs then would not fall out of first place for 155 days.

On May 13, 1969, Ernie Banks had seven RBI, including his 1,500th on a three-run homer during a 19-0 blowout of San Diego. It matched the biggest shutout margin in major league history. Cubs pitcher Dick Selma took the victory with his three-hit performance. The Cubs had obtained Selma from the Padres earlier in the season. It was the third straight shutout thrown by Cubs pitchers. Ferguson Jenkins and Ken Holtzman preceded Selma's gem.

A week later, the Cubs blanked the Dodgers 7-0 in Los Angeles behind Holtzman. It was the 12th loss in a row by the Dodgers' Don Sutton in contests against the Cubs.

On June 15, 1969, Beckert's double-play partner, Don Kessinger, set a National League record with his 54th straight errorless game to start the season. But the Cubs dropped a 7-6 decision in the first game of a doubleheader in Cincinnati.

On July 14, the Cubs edged the Mets 1-0 behind Bill Hands's win against Tom Seaver. Billy Williams singled home the game winner to give the Cubs a five and a half-game lead over the Mets. At the end of the game, Santo infuriated the Mets by jumping up and clicking his heels in glee as the Chicago crowd roared its approval.

On "Billy Williams Day" (June 29) at Wrigley Field, Williams passed Stan Musial's NL record for consecutive games played (896). The Cubs swept the Cardinals 3-1 and 12-1 in front of 41,060 fans.

In a memorable 4-3 loss to the Mets on July 8, Santo criticized center fielder Don Young for two misplays in the outfield. Santo apologized the next day for ripping into Young, who had left the park early and did not take the team bus. But Santo was booed by the home crowd in his first game back at Wrigley Field.

Holtzman pitched the fifth no-hitter in the majors of 1969 on August 19 against the Braves. Holtzman no-hit Atlanta despite failing to strikeout a single batter in the 3-0 victory. Williams hauled in a deep drive hit by Hank Aaron against the left field vines in the seventh inning to help preserve the no-hitter.

By August 27, the Cubs' lead over the Mets had slipped to two games. A 6-3 loss to the Reds was the Cubs' seventh in their last eight games.

The Cubs dropped to second place on September 10 after losing to the Phillies 6-2. The Cubs were out of first place after spending 155 days atop the National League East. Meanwhile, the Mets swept the Montreal Expos, 3-2 and 7-1, to take a one-game lead in the division.

The Cubs would continue to swoon and wound up with a 9-17 record in the month of September. Their final season record was 92-70. Jenkins would wind up with a 21-15 record and a 3.41 ERA. Hands was 20-14, 2.29. Holtzman checked in with a 17-13 record and a 3.58 ERA. Reliever Phil Regan had a 12-6 record and 17 saves.

"You have to be very lucky with the health of your team and you have to get hot the last month of the season," said Beckert. "I don't know what happened to us in '69, but we just cooled off. The whole team, we went downhill together. I was having trouble fielding. We all were. The hitting and pitching went down. But we did have a good team for more than three quarters of the year."

Where Have You Gone?

LARRY BOWA

LARRY BOWA

He will be identified forever as a key member of the Philadelphia Phillies, but Larry Bowa also carved a brief but significant niche with the Chicago Cubs in the mid-1980s.

A member of the 1984 Cubs' division championship team, Bowa was regarded as an excellent-fielding shortstop who worked hard throughout his career to improve his hitting skills.

"The thing I remember most about that [1984] season is how it brought the city together," said Bowa. "The fans were unbelievable, supportive of the ball club. I think we caught a lot of people off guard, similar to the '89 [Cubs] team. We both had the long losing streaks in spring training. There are a lot of similarities."

Certain 1984 Cubs memories left indelible marks in Bowa's mind.

"I'll always remember the game against the Cardinals when Ryno hit the two home runs off Bruce Sutter. That stands out real big," said Bowa.

"I remember going into New York for that big series. And then the big series with the Mets in Chicago when we beat Dwight Gooden. The Mets were basically the team to beat.

"I'll never forget when we went back out on the field at Wrigley after the last home game of the season, just like the Cubs did [in '89]. Another

Brace Photo

1 · LARRY BOWA · SS
Years with Cubs: 1982-85

Recorded .984 fielding percentage in 1983 • Played in 1984 NLCS •
Totaled 169 runs scored and 102 RBI with Cubs.

thing I'll never forget ... the way Sarge [Gary Matthews] had the bleacher fans saluting him. Those things you never forget about."

The Cubs won the first two games at Wrigley Field of the then best-
of-five series. Needing to win just once in San Diego, they dropped all
three. They had a 3-0 lead with Rick Sutcliffe on the mound when the
Padres rallied to win 6-3 in Game 5.

"There is no doubt that if we had been able to get back to Chicago
[in a seven-game series] we would have won," said Bowa. "The way it
happened, it was almost like they were supposed to win. The ball that
went past Ryno [for a bad-hop double by Tony Gwynn], on any other
day is an out. The ball that went under Leon Durham's glove after he had
had a great year that year...

"Sutcliffe not being able to hold a lead was a rarity. When you look
back on it, you say maybe it wasn't meant to be."

Bowa had become accustomed to being in the starting lineup
throughout most of his career with the Phillies. But the spring training
of 1985 under feisty Cubs manager Jim Frey created some fireworks. The
Cubs wanted to take a look at their young No. 1 draft pick, 22-year-old
Shawon Dunston, and the 39-year-old Bowa began feeling a bit insecure.

Bowa, who had been anointed team captain by Frey in 1984, was
suddenly blasting Frey in the media for his failure to communicate with
him about his job status in spring training.

"I have absolutely no communication with the man [Frey] at all.
None," Bowa fumed in an article in the *Chicago Tribune*. "I come to the
ballpark every day and look for my name on the board to see if I'm playing, just like a rookie. All I want to know is what my role on this team
is."

Bowa, a .261 lifetime hitter at the time, had a disappointing season
offensively for the Cubs in 1984, hitting .223 with only 17 RBIs. Yet
Bowa felt the fact that he owned the best fielding percentage of any
active shortstop made up for that.

Don Zimmer, then the Cubs' third base coach and a high school
classmate and friend of Frey's in Cincinnati, pounced on the opportunity to lambast Bowa.

During batting practice before a spring training game in Mesa,
Arizona, Zimmer read a prepared statement to a *Chicago Tribune* sportswriter, calling Bowa, "the most selfish ballplayer I have ever met. Did you
know that Larry Bowa did not speak to Ryne Sandberg for a week to 10
days last season? Well, I know it. He [Sandberg] must have been going
too good. If you can't get along with Sandberg, you can't get along with
your wife. He [Bowa] claims the manager didn't show him any respect.

Well, Bowa drove in two runs the last three months last season and the manager still played him. No respect? Bull!"

Bowa chose not to respond immediately to Zimmer's charges, but added two days later: "I could have buried him if I wanted to, but he's not worth it."

The intense rhetoric went back and forth for months, with Bowa's agent, Jack Sands of Boston, finally asking to have his client traded, preferably to Philadelphia.

Cubs general manager Dallas Green said the ball club did not feel obliged to trade Bowa. "I do not intend for this to become the focal point of this ball club, trading Larry Bowa," said Green. "I don't know that I can better the situation for a 39-year-old shortstop."

Dunston was the Cubs' opening day shortstop in 1985. But he struggled offensively and in the field, batting only .229 in April and committing seven errors in his first 14 starts. He was optioned to Triple A Iowa on May 15, 1985. He was recalled on August 13 and finished the year with a .260 batting average.

Bowa would finish his playing career in 1985 with the Mets. He held the National League record for games played at shortstop (2,222), years leading NL shortstops in fielding (6), and for fewest errors in a season of 150 or more games (9). He also holds the major league record for highest fielding percentage for a career (.980) and for a season of over 100 games (.991).

Lawrence Robert Bowa was born December 6, 1945, in Sacramento, California He was signed originally by the Phillies as an undrafted free agent out of Sacramento Community College. He made his major league debut on April 7, 1970, and wound up hitting .250 that season.

Bowa amassed 2,191 hits in 2,247 games for a .260 career average, played in five All-Star Games, five League Championship Series and with the 1980 world champions. His nine hits led all Phillies in that World Series.

On January 7, 1982, Philadelphia traded Bowa and minor league infielder Ryne Sandberg to the Cubs in exchange for veteran shortstop Ivan DeJesus.

Green, formerly the manager of the Phillies, realized he had obtained a savvy veteran in Bowa and an untapped gem in Sandberg, who would go on to win the NL Most Valuable Player award in 1984 and become one of the greatest second basemen in major league history.

"Sandberg was obviously one of our favorite people," Green says now. "He had great athleticism and he was just a solid professional that made himself into a Hall of Fame player, in my mind. He started out as a third baseman. And he was a darn good third baseman. Then we asked him to move to second and he became what I consider a Hall of Famer."

Gary Matthews was a teammate of Bowa in 1983 when the Phillies advanced to the World Series. And Matthews and Bowa were teammates with the Cubs when "Sarge" was traded to the Cubs in 1984.

"Larry has always been a proud and determined competitor and I'll always admire him for that," said Matthews. "He was one of the most dependable shortstops defensively the game has ever known. He made the routine play, and that's what you have to be able to count on from your shortstop."

As a member of the Phillies, Matthews was dubbed "Sarge" by former teammate Pete Rose when Philadelphia captured the World Series title in 1983.

"I don't think I have ever played with or against a more dedicated player than Gary Matthews. He's a very take-charge guy, that's why I named him Sarge," said Pete Rose, who played for the Phillies in '83.

When Green acquired Matthews and Bobby Dernier for the Cubs in the 1984, that club surprised the baseball world with an NL East title.

"We needed a screamer, a holler guy, a leader. When I realized we could get him from the Phillies, I couldn't say yes fast enough," said Green.

Bowa, former third base coach of American and National League teams, played from 1970-85 with Philadelphia, the Cubs and the Mets. He's currently a studio analyst for MLB Network.

Though he lacked power, Bowa hit .280 or better four times, with a high of .305 in 1975. He had 99 career homers over 16 seasons. He was a contact hitter who rarely struck out. He also stole 318 bases during his career. With Bowa at short, the Phillies won division titles from 1976 to 1978 and the world championship in 1980. Bowa had nearly 1800 hits as a member of the Phillies.

He was named manager of the San Diego Padres on October 26, 1986, replacing Steve Boros. But his overzealous style and angry approach was ineffective. He was fired May 28, 1988, after leading San Diego to a 16-30 start. He was named the Phillies' 49th manager by general manager Ed Wade on November 1, 2000. On November 14, 2001, Bowa was named National League Manager of the Year.

Bowa talked about his stint with the Cubs when his Phillies traveled to Chicago to play the White Sox in June, 2004.

"I have a daughter [Victoria] who is 20 years old and goes to Bryn Mawr. She was born here in Chicago," said Bowa. "To this day, when we come to Chicago on road trips, she comes with me because she loves the city.

"My experience with the Cubs is something that I am glad I did," said Bowa. "I was with the Philadelphia Phillies many years, but if I had to get traded somewhere, I am glad I had the experience of playing at Wrigley Field for the Cubs. I was there when things started happening [in 1984]. The attendance started getting real good and the enthusiasm in the city was really good. I think I would have been cheated if I didn't get to play at Wrigley Field."

Bowa said he and his Cubs teammates had to make an adjustment when it came to playing at Wrigley Field.

"When I played with the Cubs, there were no lights at Wrigley Field," said Bowa, recalling that lights were not installed there until 1988. "So it was almost like an everyday job. You get up in the morning, go to work and come home at about 5:30 and barbecue or whatever you want to do and get up the next day. The only drawback that I saw at that time was when we went on road trips and came back. The first two or three days back, we had trouble getting our legs under us as a team."

Finding some familiar faces from the Philadelphia organization who had begun working for the Cubs made the transition easier for Bowa back in 1983.

"The first time you get traded, it's tough," said Bowa. "You take it personally. But the way it transpired, I am glad it happened that way. And Ryne Sandberg was a Hall of Fame throw-in in the trade. I always thought Sandberg was going to be a good hitter, but I can't say I saw him hitting that many home runs. He came on to hit the most home runs of any second baseman. It was a great honor to play with him. I was very fortunate in my career to play with Ryno and Pete Rose, Mike Schmidt and Steve Carlton."

The memories of the 1984 season still give Bowa goose bumps.

"They used to play that song called 'Jump!' at Wrigley Field in 1984," said Bowa. "Whenever I hear that now, I think of '84. We had a veteran team that captured the city that year. I wish it could have ended better. Looking back, I guess it wasn't meant to be. I played in a lot of division playoff series and the World Series with the Phillies, but I think if we had gotten to the World Series with the Cubs, it might have been a bigger thrill because of how long it had been in Chicago without a trip to the World Series."

For a skinny young shortstop who many observers felt had no shot at making it in the big leagues, Bowa carved out an impressive career.

"When the Phillies first called me up to the big leagues, we were playing the Cubs our first game," said Bowa in 2004. "I remember we were facing Fergie Jenkins. I was standing on the line when we were introduced and they were playing the National Anthem. All I remember saying to myself was: 'If I can just get one year in [the big leagues].' Then after I got one year in, then I wanted five. And it just kept going. But I was just happy that first time to be able to say I was in a big-league uniform. I knew that guys who were 'good field, no hit' didn't play very long. I learned how to become a better hitter. And to this day I respect the uniform.

"The biggest problem I have today as a manager with the young players is that they don't respect the game the way they should. When you take things for granted in this sport, it will come back to haunt you. If you lose respect for the uniform or the game, you are in a lot of trouble."

Bowa said he has learned to respect the duties of a big-league manager, as well.

"You learn from your mistakes," said Bowa. "As a player you learn. As a manager when you first take over, you think you have all the answers. I remember in San Diego, I wanted to do everything. I wanted to be the pitching coach, hitting coach, outfield coach. That's not how it is done.

BILL BUCKNER

One of the most popular Chicago Cubs during the 1970s and early '80s, Bill Buckner will be forever saddled with the ignominious memory of allowing a ground ball roll through his legs while playing first base for the Boston Red Sox in the 1986 World Series.

What should be remembered most by Cubs fans is that Buckner garnered more hits in his career than all but approximately 60 players in baseball history. He also won a batting title, and he played in four decades.

Known as "Billy Buck," he played for the Los Angeles Dodgers (1969-1976), the Cubs (1977-84), the Boston Red Sox (1984-87, 1990), California Angels (1987-88) and Kansas City Royals (1988-89).

A six-foot, one-inch, 195-pound left-handed batter and thrower, Buckner was part of an impressive crop of outstanding Dodgers in the late 1960s. He joined Steve Garvey, Bill Russell, Ron Cey, Willie Crawford, Don Sutton, Von Joshua, Charlie Hough, Bobby Valentine, Joe Ferguson, Tom Paciorek, and Doyle Alexander, among others in the Dodgers' farm system.

Though he was initially an outfielder, the Dodgers tried to use Buckner at first base as well, because of his hitting prowess. Garvey and Russell were also splitting time between the outfield, third base and

Brace Photo

22 · BILL BUCKNER · 1B/OF
Years with Cubs: 1977-84

1981 All-Star • 1980 NL Batting Champion with .324 average • Led NL in Doubles in 1981 and 1983 • Had .306 average with 15 HR and 105 RBI in 1982 • Totaled 81 HR and 516 RBI with Cubs.

shortstop. In his eight seasons under former Dodgers manager Walter Alston, Buckner had three seasons as a regular, splitting time with Garvey at first and finally winding up in the outfield in 1976.

But the Dodgers were able to acquire Rick Monday from the Cubs in January, 1977. So they sent Buckner to the Cubs in the deal, which also included Ivan DeJesus. Monday joined Reggie Smith and Dusty Baker in the Dodgers' outfield under new Dodgers manager Tommy Lasorda.

With the Cubs, Buckner was converted to first base full-time.

He hit .323 his first season, and later hit .324, .311 and .306, but was unable to help the Cubs improve in the standings. Buckner won the National League batting title in 1980, edging Keith Hernandez and Garry Templeton of the Cardinals.

Buckner suffered the first of many ankle injuries that plagued his career while a member of the Cubs. Earlier, with Los Angeles, he had been a prolific base stealer, once swiping 31 bases in a season. After 1976 he never stole more than 18 and his range in the field was affected. He would begin to ground into 16-20 double plays a season, and except for 50 games in 1980, he never played much outfield again.

Buckner, rumored to be on the trading block all spring of 1984 with the Cubs, was sent to the bench and used sparingly as a pinch hitter because Leon Durham had been shifted to first from the outfield. Buckner, understandably unhappy with his part-time status, was eventually traded for future Hall of Fame pitcher Dennis Eckersley in May of 1984.

"Buckner was not very happy, as I recall," Eckersley said.

Buckner, who had a career .296 batting average coming into the 1984 season, blamed former Cubs special assistant and scout Charlie Fox for campaigning to have him traded throughout that winter. "I don't like Charlie and he doesn't like me," Buckner said.

"Buckner's paranoid," Fox replied. "Who does he think he is? Does he think his stuff doesn't stink? He's not that good."

Two years later Buckner would become part of baseball infamy when he allowed Mookie Wilson's slow ground ball to go through his legs in Game 6 of the Red Sox's World Series loss to the New York Mets.

Buckner played two full seasons with the Red Sox, in 1985 and 1986. He drove in 100 runs in both '85 and '86, batting behind Wade Boggs and in front of Jim Rice and Tony Armas. In 1986, he drove in 102 runs, even though he batted just .276 with men on base and .242 with a .340 slugging percentage with men in scoring position.

The postseason of 1986 was Buckner's worst nightmare.

He batted .200 with four RBIs in 14 games, and had just one extra-base hit. Boston manager John McNamara left him at first base in the bottom of the 10th inning of Game 6 of the World Series with a two-run lead, while defensive specialist Dave Stapleton was left on the bench. Red Sox faithful were stunned to see a ground ball roll through Buckner's legs and down the right field line, allowing the Mets' Ray Knight to score the game-winning run. The Red Sox then lost a three-run lead in Game 7. He was released by the Red Sox on July 23, 1987, to make room for prospect Sam Horn.

Buckner spent 1987, 1988 and 1989 with the Angels and then the Kansas City Royals. In 1990, the Red Sox signed him as a free agent. He played 22 games as a first baseman and pinch hitter. He even managed to hobble around the bases for an inside-the-park home run in Fenway Park. Buckner retired before the 1990 season ended. He recorded 2,715 hits, 498 doubles, 174 home runs, 183 steals, 1,077 runs scored, 1,208 RBIs and a .289 lifetime batting average.

Buckner's career did feature more pleasant postseason memories with the Los Angeles Dodgers. He appeared in the 1974 National League Championship Series and the 1974 World Series before the heartbreaking 1986 American League Championship Series and 1986 World Series with Boston.

Buckner said he was aware of some players who used steroids during his playing career.

"I know a couple guys used them later when I was playing, but just a couple," Buckner said in 2004. "I don't think the numbers [of people using them] are as high as people are talking about. You've still got to hit the ball. You can't just take steroids to get big; you have to work out, too. You look at my legs and you knew I didn't take steroids."

Buckner, who served as the hitting coach for the White Sox several years ago, says he has no immediate aspirations to get back into baseball as a manager or coach.

"This is a great place to play here and professional baseball is a great way to make a living," Buckner said in 2004. "I was very fortunate. Just right now, I like being home [in Idaho]. I had the opportunity to coach at a couple places this year. I had enough. Down the road maybe, but right now I'd rather be home with my family.

"I manage my son's team and that's enough. The 13-year-olds and dealing with their parents, that's enough."

Born December 14, 1949, in Vallejo, California, Buckner was a National League All-Star in 1981, and he visited Wrigley Field about 20 years later during an afternoon that was deemed "Bill Buckner Baseball

Card Day." Fans received the card commemorating Buckner's 1980 season with the Cubs. He threw out the first pitch and sang "Take Me Out to the Ballgame" during the seventh-inning stretch.

But he still prefers the small-town life.

"It's so different. I get claustrophobic here [in Chicago] real quick with all the people driving around," said Buckner in 2004.

"I never thought a lot of things would happen," he said. "I feel very fortunate that I was able to play as long as I did in some great cities. A lot of good things happened and I'm very thankful for that. You've got some bushes out there in center field [at Wrigley] now. I wish I had those when I played here. That's a nice background.

"I can still hit the ball," Buckner said. "I wouldn't embarrass myself and could take a decent batting practice. After that, that's about it. I can't run. I throw batting practice; that's about it. I hadn't hit for a long time, and I did it a couple months ago and hit the ball real well and it surprised me."

Where Have You Gone?

JOSE CARDENAL

One of the most colorful and spirited former Cubs players, outfielder Jose Cardenal played for nine teams during his 18-year career in the big leagues.

Born October 7, 1943, in Mantanzas, Cuba, Jose Rosario Domec Cardenal also played for the Mets, Angels, Cardinals, Brewers, Indians, Phillies, Giants and Royals.

The lithe five-foot, 10-inch, 150-pound Cardenal, who sported a fluffy Afro hairstyle by the time he joined the Cubs in 1972, played in Chicago for six seasons. As the Cubs' right fielder in 1973, he led the team in hitting (.303), doubles (33), and steals (19). Chicago baseball writers named Cardenal the "Chicago Player of the Year" that season.

He wound up his playing career from 1978-80 with the Phillies, Mets and Royals. Cardenal started two games for Kansas City in the 1980 World Series before retiring. He has since coached for the Reds, Cardinals, Yankees and Devil Rays.

"I loved playing in Chicago and at Wrigley Field," said Cardenal. "The fans were just great to me and we all had a lot of fun."

Cardenal is a cousin of former big-league shortstop Bert Campaneris. On September 8, 1965, Campaneris played all nine positions against the Angels in a promotion intended to improve attendance

Brace Photo

1 · JOSE CARDENAL · OF
Years with Cubs: 1972-77

Top ten in NL batting average in 1973 and 1975 • Sixth in NL with 182 hits in 1975 • Hit 17 HR with 70 RBI and .291 average in 1972 • Had career-high 80 RBI in 1971 • Hit career-best .317 in 1975 • Totaled 61 HR and 343 RBI with Cubs.

in Kansas City. When Campaneris took the mound in the eighth inning, the first batter he faced was Cardenal, who popped out.

Cardenal made his major league debut in 1963 with San Francisco. He was unable to become a starter in the Giants' outfield in 1964 and was traded to California. On November 29, 1967, the Indians traded outfielder Chuck Hinton to the Angels for Cardenal.

As a center fielder Cardenal led the American League in steals with 37 and patrolled the outfield with great defensive awareness. But he was traded to Cleveland after two seasons with the Angels. Cardenal paced the Indians in steals twice and tied a big-league record for outfielders by making two unassisted double plays on July 16, 1968. Cardenal became the fourth outfielder in major league history with two unassisted double plays in one season, one as he helped Cleveland to a 2-1 win over the Angels. He also pulled one off on June 8 against the Tigers.

On November 20, 1970, Cardenal was traded to the Cardinals for outfielder Vada Pinson. Cardenal hit .293 with 74 RBIs that season. In a 1971 season split between St. Louis and Milwaukee, he drove in a career-high 80 runs.

Cardenal enjoyed a highlight game on May 18, 1971, when he singled in the ninth inning to give the Cardinals a 6-5 win over the Dodgers. Playing right field, Cardenal also nailed pitcher Don Sutton at first base in the third inning on a 9-3 putout.

The Brewers traded Cardenal to the Cubs on December 3, 1971, for pitcher Jim Colborn and two other players.

Cardenal seemed to find a home with the Cubs in 1972, as he spent six seasons in Chicago and was regarded as one of the team's most popular players.

On May 3, 1972, the Cubs routed the Braves, 12-1, as Cardenal ripped a triple, double, and two singles. Ferguson Jenkins was the easy winner as Jack Billingham dropped his fourth straight decision.

Cardenal went six-for-seven at the plate, including a double and a home run, driving in four runs, as the Cubs edged the Giants 6-5 in a 14-inning first game of a doubleheader on May 2, 1976.

Cardenal was accused of using a corked bat by Pete Rose in 2001. Rose was his teammate with the 1979 Phillies.

"I did have a corked bat one time," Rose told ESPN's Jayson Stark. "You know who corked them? Jose Cardenal. I never used it in a game. But we'd come in the clubhouse in Philly, and Jose Cardenal would be corking bats. You'd hear the drill going—zizzzzzzzzzzz. But I never used none of them bats in a game."

Rose is banned from baseball for betting on games as the manager of the Cincinnati Reds.

Cardenal missed a Cubs exhibition game in 1974 when he said his eyelid was stuck shut.

The 1970s were lean years for the Cubs, as several of their star players left the game. Ernie Banks retired in 1971 after hitting 512 career home runs. Also in 1974, another future Hall of Famer, Billy Williams, was traded to the Oakland A's. In 1973, All-Star third baseman Ron Santo was traded to the crosstown White Sox. That same year, future Hall of Fame pitcher Jenkins was dealt to the Texas Rangers for two infielders, one of whom was hitting standout Bill Madlock.

Madlock went four-for-four against the Montreal Expos on October 3, 1976—the final game of the season—to clinch the National League batting crown with a .339 batting average.

During his first season with the Cubs, Cardenal watched 22-year-old teammate Burt Hooton pitch a 4-0 no-hitter against the Phillies on April 16, 1972. It was just Hooton's fourth major league start and his knuckle-curve baffled the Phils. He walked seven and struck out seven.

On April 28, 1972, Cubs first baseman Joe Pepitone returned to the lineup after being sidelined with a stomach ailment. He belted two three-run homers as the Cubs out-slugged the Reds 10-8. Cardenal and Rick Monday also homered as the Cubs captured their first win of the season in nine games. Jenkins was credited with the win. Jenkins finished the 1972 season with a 20-12 record and 3.20 earned run average.

Later that same season, Cardenal witnessed Cubs right-hander Milt Pappas throwing a no-hitter against the San Diego Padres on September 2, 1972.

Home plate umpire Bruce Froemming called a close 3-2 pitch a ball with two outs in the ninth inning to ruin the chance of a perfect game. Pappas has yet to get over that controversial call.

"That will never go away. Everytime the no-hitter and perfect game comes up... my fat buddy Bruce Froemming is still umpiring. He's still ornery. Nobody likes the guy," said Pappas in 2004.

A unique pitching gem turned in by Cubs pitchers came on August 21, 1975, when Rick and Paul Reuschel became the first brothers to combine on a shutout in the Cubs' 7-0 win over the Los Angeles Dodgers.

Cardenal had batting averages of .291, .303, .293, .317, .299 and .239 during his six seasons with the Cubs. He played under four different managers with the Cubs in six years—Leo Durocher, Whitey Lockman, Jim Marshall and Herman Franks.

The Cubs finished with an 85-70 record in 1972 under Durocher when Cardenal batted .291, but the team finished 11 games out of first place. The team would never finish above .500 during the remainder of Cardenal's stint in Chicago. They were 77-84 in 1973; 66-96 in '74; 75-87 in '75; 75-87 again in '76; and 81-81 in '77.

"Those were tough times because we were playing as hard as we could. We just couldn't get over the hump," said Cardenal. "We were always looking for the right chemistry on the team."

After the Cubs lost 22-0 to the Pittsburgh Pirates in 1975, Cardenal said: "I was watching a spider crawl through the ivy. What else was there to do out there in a game like that?"

The Cubs' opening day lineup in 1971 had Cardenal leading off and playing right field. He was followed by Glenn Beckert at second base, Billy Williams in left, Ron Santo at third, Joe Pepitone at first, Randy Hundley catching, Rick Monday in center, Don Kessinger at shortstop and Ferguson Jenkins on the mound.

Cardenal was in the opening day lineup each of the six seasons he played for the Cubs, batting leadoff in '71, second in '73, fifth in '74, and second again in '75, '76 and '77.

"I usually made good contact, but I also could hit for a little power sometimes," said Cardenal, who had 138 career homers, including a career-high 17 during his first season with the Cubs in 1972.

"You don't have to be a home run hitter to hit home runs here [at Wrigley Field]," Cardenal once said.

He was traded to the Phillies in 1978.

RON CEY

Regarded by many as the best third baseman in Los Angeles Dodgers history, Ron Cey also spent four productive seasons with the Chicago Cubs.

A member of the 1984 NL East division championship Cubs, Cey smacked 316 career homers over 17 seasons and drove in 1,139 runs.

Nicknamed "The Penguin," the five-foot, nine-inch, 185-pound Cey was drafted in the third round of the 1968 amateur draft by the Dodgers.

"Chuck Brayton, my college baseball coach [at Washington State], gave me that nickname my freshman year up there," said Cey, who also attended Western Washington State University. "It stuck. I started playing professionally two years later and Tommy Lasorda started calling me 'The Penguin.' He thought he was the originator and I had to tell him that he wasn't. I thought it was great. The kids enjoyed it. It was a popular nickname and one that was kind of endearing. Somebody else might have been offended by it, but I really didn't take it that way at all."

Cey retired in 1987 after receiving only part-time duty in Oakland.

"I do corporate entertaining and special events now for the Dodgers," said Cey in 2004. "I have been doing this the better part of five years now. I go to the suites [at Dodger Stadium] for our preferred

Brace Photo

11 · RON CEY · 3B
Years with Cubs: 1983-86

Fourth in NL with 97 RBI and fifth with 25 HR in 1984 • Had one HR and three RBI in 1984 NLCS • Totaled 84 HR and 286 RBI with Cubs

clients and our other corporate clients. I greet them and say hello to all their friends and family. Pose for pictures and talk to them all. I also go to the Stadium Club, which is one of our greeting places. And our premier ticket holders are the dugout seats where there is a private club. I spend my time kind of going back and forth between those three places. And then when the club is out of town, sometimes my job becomes community affairs and charity events. We might have a corporate client who wants to come down and have the field for a day and we will tape it."

In his final season with Oakland, Cey appeared in just 45 games and had 104 at-bats. He hit .221.

"Once I spent my last half year in Oakland, I was pretty sure I could have played a little bit longer," said Cey. "But the situation there really didn't present itself any better. I couldn't get anything done playing once a week and learning how to DH.

"Playing a little first base and third base defensively at times—the opportunities just weren't as great as I had imagined. Part of it was because of the emergence of Mark McGwire. He basically came out of nowhere. He wasn't even supposed to make the team at the time. He ended up making the final roster before the season started. The kid they had given the first base job to went into the tank just about two weeks before the end of spring training. I thought that might be an opportunity for me to play quite a bit of first base because of the circumstances. After they sent that kid down, they really gave Mark the first shot at it. It was really the right move. Then, the rest is history, as they say. It limited my playing time, it was very difficult for me at that point, and I didn't have time to really get anything established."

Born February 15, 1948, in Tacoma, Washington, Cey had spent most of his life playing baseball. He lettered in baseball, football and basketball at Mt. Tacoma High School. He was a member of the 1981 world champion Dodgers and earned World Series MVP honors. Like most professional athletes, the transition to the real world took a little time.

"When I retired, I basically became Mr. Mom for quite a while," said Cey. "For probably about five or six years, I spent a lot of time with the kids. Taking them to school, taking them to events. Just being around. And I took the time to do whatever I wanted to do for a while. Once the kids went off to school, then it opened up little bit more of an opportunity for me to branch out. Peter O'Malley came to me just before he sold the [Dodgers] team to Rubert Murdoch and Fox. He asked me to come back on some level and try to bring back some of the memories of the '70s and kind of re-create an attitude that had been missing for quite some time.

"I continued to do that with Fox, and I am continuing to do that with [current Dodgers owner] Frank McCord. At this point I am really fortunate, because I basically get to write the script. It gives me a lot of flexibility. And, yet, whatever it takes for me to get my job done is the amount of time I spend on it. It may take one day. It may take six or seven hours. It doesn't really matter, as long as I have done the job to the point where I feel I have done the best I could with it. I don't have anybody micromanaging me. So that's comfortable."

The Cubs acquired Cey in a trade with the Dodgers on January 19, 1983, in exchange for minor leaguers Vance Lovelace and Dan Cantaline. Cey was dealt to Oakland on January 30, 1987 for Luis Quinones.

"I enjoyed it [with the Cubs]," said Cey. "It wasn't exactly a great start. Opening day in 1983, we were getting lined up, being introduced at home, and it starts snowing. That's kind of the way things went, I think, until June. We got snowed out in Pittsburgh, Philadelphia, at home. It was miserable weather. I didn't adjust to it very well. I may have had one home run [by] June. And I may have been hitting below .200. But in the end, it got straightened out. And I ended up hitting 20-some [24] home runs and 90 RBIs. I led the club in home runs and RBIs. Then the next year, Dallas [Green] did a real good job of putting this team even further together. We really had a nice rotation with Scott Sanderson, Rick Sutcliffe, Dennis Eckersley and Steve Trout. We had a good closer in Lee Smith.

"The bullpen was solid with Tim Stoddard and Warren Brusstar and Ray Fontenot and a few others. And the everyday lineup was solid. We got some real good years, a career year from Jody Davis in 1984. Ryne Sandberg was the MVP. Bobby Dernier, Keith Moreland and Gary Matthews all did a great job in the outfield. Leon Durham was right behind me in RBIs. I think he had 96 and I had 97. And Larry Bowa did his job at shortstop.

"We got into the playoffs and we were cruising. All of a sudden a little ground ball gets away [under Durham] and the series is over with," said Cey. "It was tough, but we did have a great time that year. We were able to get Chicago on the map, and we brought a lot of fans to the ballpark. We had a good time together.

"In 1985, unfortunately we couldn't get back to where we were the year before. We lost all of our [starting] pitchers within a month's span," said Cey. "We just couldn't replace those guys. That put a lot of stress on the offense. It seemed like we had to score 10 runs every day just to be in the game. Of course, that wasn't the case, necessarily, but it felt like it."

Cey split time at third base with Moreland in 1986. He had 13 homers in 97 games.

"In 1986, they just started dismantling the team a little bit," said Cey. "In my last year, I don't think I got more than 250 at-bats. But I felt it was really productive. It would have probably translated into about 25 home runs and close to 90 RBIs and 40-some doubles. It would have been a good, full year if Jim Frey had elected to play me a little bit more. But I knew I was on the way out. I went to Oakland."

Cey was paid $1.45 million by the Cubs in 1985, which included a unique attendance clause. The Cubs drew a then club-record 2,161,534 fans to Wrigley Field in 1985.

"Dallas Green basically told me when we were negotiating to come to Chicago [in '82], that he was going to bring in a lot of people and he was going to make things happen in a short period of time," said Cey. "You are a little bit reluctant and skeptical in the beginning. Because I hadn't been in that position before. And sure enough, he did it. Much to his credit, he turned things around. With the exception of all the injuries in '85, I think we would have won the division title again. We were cruising along pretty good. We got hit in the face with injuries in June.

"Dallas was trying to control the payroll [with incentive clauses]," said Cey. "Because I was going to be the highest-salaried player there, he didn't want to jack it up far over the top. He was convinced that things would work because of the [personnel] changes and we were going to get a winner in here. We both thought the attendance levels were really going to pick up. I felt this was a different type of an opportunity. And I was willing to roll with it. That's how it came out. Dallas was trying to put just about everybody who had a contract on some kind of incentive clause.

"A lot of the pitchers and a lot of the utility players all had incentives for at-bats, games played, innings pitched, all that stuff," said Cey. "I really wasn't for any of that. I felt like you signed a contract to play 162 games and I wanted to play as many of them as I can.

"At the end of 1985, all of those guys who were closing in on incentives got nixed," said Cey. "Many of them were very unhappy about that. I remember going into St. Louis for the last game of the season. We have called up Greg Maddux, we've called up Greg Moyer, we've called up Joe Carter, we've called up Rafael Palmiero. We have called up all these kids. And they were all playing for the most part.

"Now we come to St. Louis and Jim Frey comes to me before the last game of the season and tells me that I have to play that day," said Cey. "I don't even remember the last time I had played before that. Frey said, 'Hey, look, I don't want to be the bad guy here, but Dallas Green has informed me that there are a number of guys on this team who are on the bubble [for incentives] and they need to sit this game out. The year hasn't been successful and they don't want to pay any more money out.'

"By me playing, that took Chris Speier right out of the picture. He only needed an at-bat or two. I think Lee Smith got axed, too. All of those who were on the bubble got axed. I felt badly. I went over and talked to Chris and said, 'You know, I really feel bad about this. Frey has told me that I am starting today. I don't have anything to do with this.'

"Chris said, 'Don't worry about it. I completely understand. Don't worry about it as far as you and I are concerned. We're cool.' But I really felt bad. That's where you have a situation where the club could manipulate the contracts that are under those types of incentives. That's why I didn't want to be involved with those."

All in all, Cey said he enjoyed his experience with the Cubs.

"My job was to drive in runs. It didn't matter how I was going to do it," he said.

JODY DAVIS

"**J**ody! Jody Davis…!"

That was the familiar, if not slightly off-key, refrain of legendary broadcaster Harry Caray every time the Cubs' catcher would step to the plate. Davis was one of the more popular players among Cubs fans as well.

A Georgia native, Davis returned to his roots following his retirement from baseball.

"Then I went to work in the auto racing field down there," Davis said several years ago before greeting well-wishers at a Cubs Fans Convention in Chicago. "I was working with Dale Earnhardt. I really enjoyed it. Now that he's gone, I have to look for something else."

Davis played for the Cubs from 1981-87. In 1988 he was traded to the Atlanta Braves because the Cubs were impressed with young catcher Damon Berryhill. Davis had hit a career-low .230 in 1987.

Originally drafted by the New York Mets, Davis was traded to the St. Louis Cardinals organization for Ray Searage following the 1979 season. Davis played in 58 games for the Cardinals in 1980. He was treated for an ulcer, lost 50 pounds and nearly died during the ordeal. He was picked up by the Cubs on December 8, 1980, when he was drafted off

Brace Photo

7 · JODY DAVIS · C
Years with Cubs: 1981-88

Two-time All-Star • 1986 NL Gold Glove Award • Had career-best .271 with 24 HR in 1983 • Had career-high 94 RBI in 1984 • Hit .389 with 2 HR and 6 RBI in 1984 NLCS • Totaled 122 HR and 467 RBI with Cubs

the roster of the Triple A Springfield Redbirds of the St. Louis organization.

Davis started out with a bang as a member of the Cubs, hitting .389 in the month of May in 1981. But Keith Moreland won the job from him the following spring training, before Davis took over again during the 1982 season. Moreland, who was later switched to the outfield, would become one of Davis's best friends over the years.

In 1983 Davis hit .271 with 24 homers and 84 RBIs. In 1984 he made the National League All-Star team for the first time as the Cubs won the NL East, and he enjoyed a 15-game hitting streak. He had 94 RBIs that season. Only Hall of Famer Gabby Hartnett had driven in more runs as catcher in franchise history.

Davis starred in the '84 NLCS, with seven hits in five games and home runs in Games 4 and 5. But the Cubs lost the final three games to the Padres after taking a 2-0 series lead.

On June 10, 1984, the typically slow afoot catcher was actually part of a triple steal. Leon Durham stole home while Davis took third and Larry Bowa went to second in the ninth inning as the Cubs beat the Cardinals' Joaquin Andujar 2-0.

Davis was afflicted with an intestinal virus in 1985, forcing him to miss a crucial part of the season, when the Cubs lost 13 games in a row. The Cubs fell precipitously from first place in early June to fifth place and 23 1/2 games out of first by the end of the season.

The entire Cubs starting pitching staff spent time on the disabled list in 1985, as well as center fielder Bobby Dernier and several other key performers.

The four original starting pitchers—Rick Sutcliffe, Dennis Eckersley, Steve Trout and Scott Sanderson—missed a total of 52 starts. All four were on the disabled list in August. Dick Ruthven, the fifth starter, missed nine starts. The Cubs lost another 242 games from position players because of injuries.

Davis was hitting .273 with six homers and 25 RBIs on June 11, 1985. He finished with a .232 average, 17 homers and 58 RBIs.

"I always felt like I had the flu that year," said Davis. "I was feeling run down, yet I was still playing. I just decided one day to tell somebody that something wasn't right. We were in New York and [trainer] Tony Garofalo sent me to see the Mets' doctor. At first he told me I had some type of virus. That's when we found out my blood count was low and I was bleeding [internally]."

Davis left the club on June 21 in St. Louis and returned to Chicago to be hospitalized. He rejoined his teammates on June 29 in Pittsburgh, but hit only .200 in July with three homers and 13 RBIs.

"I got ahold of some aspirin that tore up my stomach and caused some internal bleeding," said Davis during spring training of 1986. "If I stay away from the aspirin, I should be healthy."

The disappointment of the 1985 season was felt throughout the city of Chicago. The Cubs drew a record attendance in '85. They set a city and franchise attendance record by drawing 2,161,534 paid fans to Wrigley Field. They also led the National League in road attendance by attracting a club-record of 2,255,306.

Davis signed a three-year contract worth nearly $3 million with incentive clauses just before the 1986 season.

Future Hall of Famer Gary Carter, then of the New York Mets, and Tony Pena, with the Pirates that season, were the only catchers in the National League who were being paid more than Davis.

As the wear and tear of catching began to take its toll, Davis started thinking about prolonging his career before the '86 season began.

"As far as getting tired, I think I'd like to catch only about 135 games a year," he said then. "That sounds like a number that is ideal for me, unless we're in the thick of the race at the end of the season, and then you've got to go.

"This is only my sixth year in the big leagues," Davis said in '86, "and I don't have too many aches and pains. But one thing I do notice…when I'm hunting in the winter and sitting real still, my knees start to ache a little bit."

Davis theorized that he could be doing other valuable duties for the Cubs when he was not catching.

"I could pinch hit and maybe play some first base," he said. "I played a lot of first base in American Legion ball and in high school and in the minor leagues. I played first base way before I ever caught. I have mentioned that to [Cubs manager] Jim Frey. But every time I say something to him about it, he just laughs. I can play first base, too. I just don't think Jim thinks I can."

Frey said he would rather see Davis try to improve his defensive skills behind the plate instead of looking for ways to move to first base. Davis threw out 46 of 161 runners [28 percent] attempting to steal in 1985, while being charged with 14 passed balls and eight errors in 786 chances for a .990 fielding percentage.

Johnny Oates, the Cubs' bullpen coach in 1986, spent many hours working with Davis and backup catcher Steve Lake on their defensive techniques.

"I feel like I had a pretty good year defensively, considering all the different pitchers throwing to me," said Davis, referring to the minor leaguers called up when the starters were hurt in 1985. "It's tough catching guys that you have to introduce yourself to before the game. You don't have any idea what they want to throw or what they want to try to do. Everybody on this team feels like we were embarrassed. My big thing is home runs and RBIs. I'd like to hit 25 or 30 home runs and drive in 100 to 115 runs. But I guess the ultimate goal is winning that World Series ring."

Sure enough, Davis won a Gold Glove in 1986, throwing out 78 would-be base stealers. He also hit 21 home runs. But in 1987 his production started to slip. He had caught at least 138 games each of the previous four seasons and had never gone on a major league disabled list. But in 1988 an early-season stint on the DL forced the promotion of Berryhill from the minors, and Davis would catch only 76 games.

The Cubs traded Davis to the Braves for pitchers Kevin Coffman and Kevin Blankenship on September 29, 1988.

Davis was a .246 career hitter with 127 home runs and 489 RBIs in 1,075 games.

Born Jody Richard Davis in Gainesville, Georgia, on November 12, 1956, Davis attended North Hall High School in Gainesville and earned four letters in baseball and three in basketball before graduating in 1975. He was All-State in basketball his senior year. Davis attended Middle Georgia College in Cochran, Georgia, for one year. He was selected by the Mets in the third round of the June, 1976, amateur free agent draft.

In 1984, Davis hit .256 with 19 homers. But his biggest contribution was handling a pitching staff that was the surprise of the league and nearly made it to the World Series.

Sutcliffe jumped into the arms of Davis when he beat the Pirates 4-1 in 1984 to clinch the NL East title. Sutcliffe, with his 14th straight triumph, earned his 20th victory of the season overall, becoming only the fourth pitcher in major league history to accomplish the feat while crossing leagues. He improved his record to 16-1 with the Cubs, after going 4-5 with Cleveland, making him the first 20-game winner in the majors in 1984.

ANDRE DAWSON

Andre Dawson was finally formally recognized for his stellar playing career in 2011 when he was enshrined in the Baseball Hall of Fame with 77.9 percent of the vote.

Dawson always prided himself on being a patient man, but he regretted the fact that his late mother—Mattie Brown—was not alive to see him receiving baseball's ultimate recognition.

"She always told me that [the Hall of Fame] was inevitable. Just be patient and keep the faith. That's why it is so disheartening for me that she is not here to experience that, because I know how proud she would have been," he said.

Dawson's former teammates were just as happy as he was when the Hall of Fame honor was bestowed.

"Shawon Dunston called and was crying. He had me crying, listening to the message," said Dawson. "I talked to Ryno [Ryne Sandberg]. I talked to some of my teammates from other teams; I talked to managers, coaches: Jose Martinez, Zim [Don Zimmer], Dick Williams. I am thrilled that all of these individuals have reached out to me. I had over 100 text messages and 60 voice messages before I could even reply to one of them. My phone went dead at one point. It is such a tremendous feeling."

Brace Photo

8 · ANDRE DAWSON · OF
Years with Cubs: 1987-92

Five-time All-Star • 1987 NL MVP • 1987 and 1988 NL Gold Glove
Award • Led MLB with 49 HR and 137 RBI in 1987 • Played in 1989
NLCS • Totaled 174 HR and 587 RBI with Cubs

Dawson, nicknamed "The Hawk," wound up with 438 career home runs, a .279 batting average and eight Gold Gloves during his 21-year career. He persevered in spite of two chronically injured knees that required daily medical attention during his final years.

"I always played the game, I don't want to say with reckless abandon, but I would always leave everything out on the field," said Dawson. "I tried not to let one aspect of the game overrule the other. I would have years in which I would hit for higher average and less power. And I would hit for more power in other years and the average would be down. A lot of that has to do with what is surrounding you and what kind of start you get off to. Or the way you are pitched that particular year. But I just tried to be a five-tool player."

Dawson starred for the Expos, Cubs, Red Sox and Marlins, winning the NL Most Valuable Player award in 1987 after hitting 49 homers and driving in 137 runs for the last-place Cubs. He hit for the cycle on April 29, 1987.

He began his career with Montreal, where he was voted NL Rookie of the Year in 1977. He was an Expos teammate of Pete Rose in 1984.

"I think definitely [Rose] belongs in the Hall of Fame," said Dawson in 2004 of the all-time hits leader who has admitted to betting on baseball. "Whether he is in a position to return to baseball in some capacity or the other, I think that should be judged a little bit differently. What he did out on the field merits him being in the Hall of Fame. That has always been my stance. Pete Rose undoubtedly is a Hall of Famer."

Dawson said Rose kept his apparent gambling addiction under wraps with the Expos.

"I never knew that he was a big-time gambler when we played together in Montreal," said Dawson. "I can only recall one incident when we went to the dog tracks in St. Pete [Florida]. I went with Pete and a couple of other players. I am not a gambler. I am not a risk taker at all. I think I may have bet $50, and that was a portion of my meal money. I went for the entertainment part of it. But none of us was aware that Pete was a big-time gambler."

One of Dawson's closest friends has been former Expos teammate Tim Raines, who battled a cocaine addiction during the '80s. Dawson represented a big brother figure as Raines sought treatment and counseling.

Dawson views Rose's gambling problem as another type of addiction.

"Any time you get caught up in a distraction like that and it pretty much consumes you, it is [an addiction]," said Dawson. "Anytime it just takes control of you, it's an addiction. I don't want to call it a sickness or illness, but it is a form of an addiction. I think Pete got a form of satisfaction out of [gambling] and didn't look at it as a gambling problem. Maybe for him it was a form of recreation. He had so much money and he didn't know what to do with it. I think it was wrong if he did bet on baseball. But I think that should be judged separately from what he did on the field. When he put that uniform on, he was a different individual, and one of the better people you would ever want to meet on the playing field."

Before Sammy Sosa joined the Cubs, the fan favorite of the Wrigley Field bleacherites was Dawson. "The Hawk" wound up with the enduring respect of his fans.

Dawson, now 58, works with the Marlins.

"I am special assistant to the president [of the Marlins]," Dawson said. "And what it entails is that I work on the field in spring training. I don't travel that much, but I may be with the club on a road trip or two. I do some community work and I just have to be available for certain things."

Dawson played the game with so much enthusiasm, dedication and respect that it bothers him to see many star players today conduct themselves so selfishly.

"The game has changed so much," he said. "I think finances have changed the attitude of the players a great deal—the way that they conduct themselves, not only on the field but off the field. Of course, there is reason to take note and be concerned about it. Hopefully, this won't in the end destroy the game, because we have enough problems as it is. The players who go around thinking they are bigger than the game itself need to change."

Cubs fans, especially the ones in the Wrigley Field right field bleachers, used to bow toward Dawson in respect when he took his position after hitting a home run.

"My six years with the Cubs [1987-92] pretty much got my career rejuvenated. As far as I am concerned, there is no better place to play. People always talk about New York, but I never had any aspirations to play there. But to come to Chicago...the warmth of the Friendly Confines and the knowledge of the fans...the thing that they do best is allow you to enjoy yourself and have fun. The pressure should be on the front office to get the right personnel on the field. As far as the fans are concerned, they are very accommodating and I just want them to get what they deserve," said Dawson.

Fans and media will never forget seeing Dawson at spring training in Mesa, Arizona, in 1987. He and his agent, Dick Moss, presented the Cubs a blank contract when he was a free agent leaving Montreal. Former Cubs general manager Dallas Green referred to that scene as a "dog and pony show." But Dawson was sincere.

"If I had to do it all over again, I probably would do it the same way. It was just a matter, for me, of going somewhere that I knew I would enjoy the game and be a little more respected from a management standpoint," said Dawson.

"I couldn't have picked a better place. I always loved daytime baseball and I always enjoyed playing in Wrigley Field. If I had to do it again I probably would tell them they couldn't pay me enough."

His first season with the Cubs, Dawson hit 49 home runs and drove in 137 runs to earn the league MVP award. But the enduring image of him was watching him painstakingly ice his knees after every game.

"They haven't gotten any better. I am looking at knee replacement down the road," said the Hawk in 2004.

Per custom for Hall of Fame ballplayers, Dawson and his wife, Vanessa, were given a guided tour of the Hall of Fame Museum in Cooperstown, N.Y., months before the actual July 25, 2011 induction ceremony.

Showing the enthusiasm and bright smile of a youngster, Dawson grabbed one of the bats displayed that Babe Ruth used 80 years earlier.

"I could have swung this," Dawson said as he admired the finely-carved wood and sturdy grip.

The tour included close-up views of the Hall of Fame plaques of former Cubs Ernie Banks, Billy Williams, Fergie Jenkins and Ryne Sandberg, and Dawson wondered if his plaque would depict him with or without a mustache.

With special interest, Dawson gazed at the detailed exhibits of Hank Aaron, Lou Gehrig, Willie Mays, Cy Young and many others.

"When I walk through this gallery, I feel like I'm on sacred ground. You're talking about the greatest players ever to play the game, some of which I had the opportunity to see play, to play against, and others I read the history of," he said during the tour. "I can't begin to say enough about how exhilarating the feeling is just to walk into the Hall of Fame... let alone take a tour and learn the history about all of these great players."

When Sandberg was inducted into the Hall of Fame five years earlier, the stellar second baseman made a point of lobbying for Dawson during his induction speech, saying that Dawson played the game "the right way."

"Obviously it was a huge endorsement, coming from one of my peers, one of my teammates... an individual I hold high esteem and respect for as a teammate," Dawson said before his induction.

Dawson always was mindful of the importance of the fans, wherever he played.

"I got my start in Montreal, and the game still was new to the city," said Dawson. "They were still learning the game, but they were very supportive. They knew how to enjoy the game and never really put any pressure on me. I was there for 10 years, and playing across the border was quite the experience... a different culture, learning a lot of different things about that country. Playing in Chicago... the fans just gave me a new vision on my career, embracing me from day one. And allowing me to really enjoy the game in, perhaps, a media center such as Chicago. Being able to sit out and listen to Harry Caray every day... have five to 10 thousand sunbathers out there in right field [bleachers], salamming me... that place overwhelmed me to the extent that I couldn't wait to get to the ballpark every day. I owe a great deal to the fans. The fans are what fueled me. Not numbers, not statistics. But the fans because, to me, they were that extra energy."

BOBBY DERNIER

The front half of the Daily Double, Bobby Dernier was a resourceful leadoff man who set the table for league MVP Ryne Sandberg during the Cubs' 1984 NL East division championship campaign.

"It was a fun season I was a part of," said Dernier, who now lives in Kansas City and has been involved in a baseball training academy for several years. "There were too many memories in a long season like that to pick one."

Acquired from the Philadelphia Phillies along with leftfielder Gary Matthews on March 26, 1984, Dernier added spark and confidence to a unit unaccustomed to such bravado.

The regular season for the 1984 Cubs defied all odds as they wound up with a 96-65 record and drew two million fans (2,107,655) for the first time in franchise history. The Cubs had finished fifth the previous season with an abysmal 77-84 record. The Cubs lost 11 straight exhibition games in the spring of '84 and finished with the worst preseason record (7-20) in all of baseball. Then they suddenly ruled their division.

"I've got a plan," first-year Cubs manager Jim Frey proclaimed that spring training during the 11-game losing streak. Frey, called Preacher Man by the players such as Dernier behind his back, didn't know then how prophetic his statement would be.

Brace Photo

20 · BOBBY DERNIER · OF
Years with Cubs: 1984-87

1984 NL Gold Glove Award • Scored 94 runs and stole 45 bases in 1984 • Had 1 HR and 2 SB in 1984 NLCS • Hit .317 in 1987 • Stole 119 bases with Cubs

Dernier, the Cubs' lithe center fielder, hit .278 and stole a club-high 45 bases in his first full major league season in 1984. He also set career highs with 149 hits, 94 runs, 26 doubles and 32 RBIs.

After starting the 1985 season on the right foot, he had to be placed on the 15-day disabled list on June 15 with an injury to his left foot. He had to be operated on by team surgeon Dr. Michael Schafer. There was a knot on the top of his left foot, described as ganglion nerve tissue. Dernier apparently broke a bone in his foot unknowingly when he was with the Phillies organization in 1982.

"I was trying to play through this injury and I was slowed down to a jog," said Dernier. The Cubs called up rookie Darrin Jackson from Class Double A Pittsfield, Mass., to take Dernier's roster spot.

After coming so tantalizingly close to advancing to the World Series in 1984, the Cubs would finish 23 1/2 games out of first place in 1985.

The Cubs opened the '85 season optimistically. They were 15 games over .500 at 34-19 and in first place during the first week of June. But in addition to Dernier, Cy Young Award-winning pitcher Rick Sutcliffe spent three tours on the disabled list in '85, as did the entire starting pitching staff of Scott Sanderson, Dick Ruthven, Steve Trout and Dennis Eckersley.

The Cubs lost another 242 games from position players because of injuries in 1985.

Dernier, who missed over a month with his foot injury in '85, reported to spring training in 1986 wearing a softer, more comfortable pair of shoes.

"I'm ready to dance with this new pair of house slippers," he quipped. "I'll be able to cover ground in center field like a blanket."

Dernier says he still gets goose bumps when he thinks of the home run he hit to lead off the '84 playoffs at Wrigley Field against the San Diego Padres.

Dernier and Sandberg were dubbed the "The Daily Double" by Hall of Fame broadcaster Harry Caray. Dernier typically would get on base with a walk or base hit and Sandberg would move him to third with a single on a hit-and-run.

Dernier was about to be sent down to the Phillies' Triple A Portland Beavers before being dealt to the Cubs.

"When Dernier got the word we had been traded to the Cubs, he called me up and sounded so excited," said Matthews. "He said: 'Gary, you're coming with me to Chicago.' I said: 'No, Bobby, you're coming to Chicago with ME.'"

The Cubs gave up 37-year-old reliever Bill Campbell and minor league catcher Mike Diaz in order to acquire Dernier and Matthews.

A native of Independence, Missouri, Dernier came to the Cubs' camp in Mesa, Arizona, with enough confidence to silence the team's incumbent center fielder Mel Hall, who had been talking trash when the Dernier trade had been announced.

"Who is this Bobby Dernier? He's not going to come in here and take my job. As far as taking my job, well...Bobby Dernier doesn't qualify, gentlemen," Hall told reporters at the Cubs spring training site.

"There were some times early on when Mel gave me a lot of stuff," said Dernier. "But I finally had to pull him aside and tell him, 'Hey, look, we've got to be professional about this. I play my game on the field, not in the clubhouse. So let's cut this crap out.' After that, we had no problems."

Hall was eventually traded to the Cleveland Indians in a controversial deal on June 13, 1984. Rookie outfield prospect Joe Carter and two minor leaguers also headed for Cleveland in exchange for pitchers Sutcliffe and George Frazier and catcher Ron Hassey.

Hall would not leave quietly, though. The Cubs' front office neglected to obtain waivers on Hall and Carter, meaning those two players were unable to play for the Indians for a five-day period. Facing the prospect of returning to the Cubs if another team had claimed him on waivers, Hall blasted the Cubs organization for dealing him.

"Who is Rick Sutcliffe?" Hall ranted in a familiar refrain. "I hope I face him sometime."

After starting the season 4-5 with Cleveland, Sutcliffe was 16-1 with the Cubs, including a club-record 14 straight regular-season victories en route to winning the NL Cy Young Award.

Dernier and Matthews had forged a solid friendship from their days in Philadelphia together. During the Phillies' pennant-winning season of 1983, Dernier played in 122 games with the big club after starting the season in the minors at Class Double A Reading.

"You can tell how so many guys rallied around the one guy who gives them the extra juice and boost every day," Dernier said of Matthews. "He's good people to talk to and learn from. He's got good manners, good etiquette, both on the field and off. I had a lot to learn in that department. None of us are angels."

Dernier also credits Matthews for teaching him how to enjoy life to the fullest.

"An example of the class that Gary demonstrates was in 1983 when we were in the World Series with the Phillies and we were going to

Baltimore," said Denier. "Gary had the limos waiting for us. We weren't going to take the bus or anything. Gary did the same thing in '84 with the Cubs when we were in the playoffs. His theme constantly was: 'You're going to go out and play hard and play to win, so go out and have fun doing it. Do it right. If you do get beat, you still will have had fun instead of drowning in your sorrows.'"

Former Cubs president/general manager Dallas Green saw the Matthews-Dernier trade as the key to the season.

"The Sutcliffe trade was great, especially for that time of the year," said Green. "But for me, the thing that got it started was Matthews and Dernier. By the time Sutcliffe and the rest of those guys got here, we could have been in last place. Matthews and Dernier got us juiced up, and it sent a message to the ball club, 'Hey, guys, we ain't fooling around here. If you don't pay attention to the job, we're going to get people who do.'"

Sandberg, then 24, was the NL Most Valuable Player in 1984, hitting .314 with a league-high 114 runs scored, 36 doubles, 19 homers and a .520 slugging percentage.

The Cubs clinched the division title in Pittsburgh's Three Rivers Stadium.

"This is only perfect; it doesn't get any better than this," said Dernier in the champagne-drenched lockerroom. "This surpasses everything. To be able to win it, with this bunch of guys. I'll go to war with these guys."

The 1984 Cubs won the first two games against the San Diego Padres at Wrigley Field of the then best-of-five National League Championship Series. Needing to win just once in San Diego, they dropped all three. The Cubs had a 3-0 lead with Sutcliffe on the mound when the Padres rallied to win 6-3 in Game 5.

Dernier now feels the Cubs would have prevailed against the Padres in '84 if the NLCS playoffs had been seven games instead of five.

"It would have been nice to have Games 6 and 7 in ChiTown," said Dernier. "They went to seven games the next year. The one thing I'll always remember was the scene of gloom on Monday [coming back to Chicago from San Diego]. Unfortunately, that's the real memory. But there were too many good ones to just dwell on that.

"I remember when we got back to Chicago after losing that last playoff game and it was raining. Then the next day we were walking out of the hotel. It was like a ghost town. It was like everybody had just died...together. But when you think about all the wins we had that year, the loss represented just another brick to build on. Like Gary Matthews said: 'Some days the best you can do isn't very good.'"

SHAWON DUNSTON

A No. 1 overall draft pick in 1982, Shawon Donnell Dunston arrived in the big leagues as a raw but abundantly talented shortstop.

The popular and electrifying Cubs standout played 18 years in the major leagues, culminating with a World Series appearance with Dusty Baker's San Francisco Giants in 2002. He spent his first 11 years with the Cubs, beginning in 1985, then once again in 1997.

A .269 career hitter, Dunston was a free swinger who never walked more than 30 times in an entire season. In fact, there were four seasons when he failed to draw a single base on balls. He struck out a total of 1,000 times in his career and walked 203 times. Blessed with a strong arm, Dunston was capable of gunning down swift base runners from deep in the hole at shortstop. He also played center field toward the end of his career.

Dunston enjoyed his first year of retirement in the Bay Area in 2003.

"I am just enjoying life. I am happy to be a father and a husband. And I am back to being normal," Dunston said. "I appreciate what the game has done for me and my family. I am stress-free, put it that way. When the cheering stops, I know I always have my family. I have three daughters—Jasmine, Whitney and I'sha. My son is Shawon, Jr."

So what kind of a ballplayer is Shawon, Jr.?

Brace Photo

12 · SHAWON DUNSTON · SS
Years with Cubs: 1985-95, 1997

**Two-time All-Star • Had 37 doubles in 1986 • Hit .316 in 1989 NLCS •
Was drafted first overall by Cubs in 1982 amateur draft • Totaled 98 HR
and 448 RBI with Cubs**

"He's pretty good. He hits left-handed, but I make him throw right-handed," said Shawon in 2004. "He is very patient at the plate. He didn't get that from me. I say, 'Why don't you swing at that pitch?' He says, 'I only swing at strikes.'"

Dunston served as a "guest coach" for current Cubs manager Dusty Baker during spring training of 2004.

Dunston was the top overall pick in the 1982 amateur draft after graduating from Thomas Jefferson High School in Brooklyn, where he stole 37 of 37 bases in his senior year and batted .790.

Born March 21, 1963, the 6'1", 180-pounder also was a dominating pitcher at that level. Dunston recalled the most exciting year for him with the Cubs.

"It was 1989. That's when we won the division. We lost in the playoffs to the Giants. They had a veteran team and we had a young team," he said.

Dunston played for St. Louis, Cleveland, the New York Mets and Pittsburgh, as well as San Francisco and the Cubs. He played in the postseason for the Cubs, Mets, Cardinals and Giants and had a .275 batting average. He appreciated the spirit and enthusiasm of baseball fans everywhere.

"Chicago is the best, easily," he said when asked to rank them. "I know Cub fans don't want to hear it, but St. Louis is a very nice place to play. Those cities are one-two." Dunston played for the Cardinals in 1999 and 2000. He returned to the Giants as a free agent on December 8, 2000, for $600,000, where he finished up his career.

During his retirement, Dunston has not been able to stay in touch with many of his former teammates.

"The only one I really stay in touch with is Eric Davis because we are both retired," Dunston said in 2004. "He laughs at me. He says: 'How are you doing at home? Are you getting on everybody's nerves?' I say, 'Yeah, how did you know?' He just starts laughing. I also stay in touch with Kenny Lofton. But I don't like to bother players who are playing right now, because I know how it is."

Dunston, who missed almost two full months of the 1994 season due to back surgery, rebounded with his best offensive season in 1995. He hit .296 with 14 homers, 30 doubles, six triples and 69 RBIs for the Cubs.

Dunston was granted free agency by the Cubs on October 31, 1995. He signed with the Giants on January 9, 1996.

A resident of Fremont, California, Dunston was drawn to the Bay Area ball club, even though the Philadelphia Phillies and Cincinnati

Reds offered him more money and more contract years. And the Chicago White Sox even talked to him about playing left field.

After one season in San Francisco, he returned to the Cubs as a free agent in Decemeber 2, 1996. A year later, Dunston was sent packing to Pittsburgh as part of a conditional deal. At the end of that season, he again became a free agent and signed with Cleveland on February 16, 1998.

Dunston, who was a member of the National League All-Star teams in 1988 and 1990 while a member of the Cubs, was acquired a second time by the Giants from the Cleveland Indians on July 23, 1998, along with reliever Jose Mesa and Alvin Morman, for pitcher Steve Reed and outfielder Jacob Cruz.

Even after the Cubs let him walk as a free agent, Dunston seemed to maintain his allegiance to the team that originally signed him. His highest yearly salary came with the Cubs in 1993 when he earned $3,775,000.

When he joined the Giants, for instance, Dunston said he received a shipment of Mark Grace's bats that helped him get out of a slump.

"I have WGN-TV. I watch the Cubs during the day and then go out and play at night," said Dunston when he was playing on the West Coast. "It's funny to see my [Cubs] uniform number (12) on Leo Gomez. At times, I find myself putting No. 12 on my back. But I'm No. 21 now with the Giants. I'm always telling Cub stories, and Matt Williams says: 'Cut the cord.'"

Dunston said there was no semblance of the Wrigley Field "Shawon-o-meter" (updating his batting average) at Candlestick Park. "All they had was a 'Shawon Dunston Growth Chart' giveaway, pointing out all the injuries I have all over my body," he said with a laugh.

Dunston bemoaned the fact that former Cubs general manager Larry Himes "didn't believe how bad my back injury was. The old regime thought I was taking too long to come back. That bothered me. Other than that, I have nothing negative to say about the Cubs organization."

Since the days of Hall of Famer Ernie Banks, the Cubs have not exactly enjoyed much stability at the shortstop position. In fact, while the Baltimore Orioles' Cal Ripken, Jr., was setting a record for consecutive games played, here are the shortstops who played for the Cubs: Larry Bowa, Dave Owen, Tom Veryzer, Dunston, Chris Speier, Mike Brumley, Paul Noce, Luis Quinones, Manny Trillo, Angel Salazar, Scott Fletcher, Junior Kennedy, Domingo Ramos, Greg Smith, Jose Vizcaino, Rey Sanchez, Luis Salazar, Alex Arias, Jeff Kunkel and Jose Hernandez.

A fierce competitor, Dunston often let his emotions of the moment get the best of him.

For instance, Dunston and Ed Lynch had to be separated on the team bus in Montreal. Lynch, who later would become the Cubs' general manager, had angered Dunston by failing to retaliate when Expos pitcher Dennis Martinez plunked him with a high hard one.

When Dunston arrived at the Cubs' spring training camp in Mesa, Arizona, in 1984, the team's first-year manager, Jim Frey, gave him the bulk of playing time. That aggravated veteran shortstop and team captain Larry Bowa to no end. Bowa feuded with Frey and Cubs third base coach Don Zimmer that spring. Dunston and Bowa would split playing time during the season, and the Cubs surprised the baseball world by winning the NL East title. The Cubs won the first two games of the best-of-five NLCS against the San Diego Padres. But the Padres won three straight at Jack Murphy Stadium in San Diego to advance to the World Series.

In the meantime, Dunston keeps an eye on the team that drafted him out of high school in 1982.

But Dunston said nothing compares to the joy of being with his family. His wife, Tracie, and the kids always come first.

"When I get old, I want to look back and say I enjoyed it with them," he said in 2004. "Daddy's got to do his job, Mommy's got to do her job. And that's even harder than mine. She's got to get the kids to school, make them do their homework. I wouldn't mind switching. Her job is worth more than millions of dollars."

Dunston is now a special assistant for the Giants.

Where Have You Gone?

LEON DURHAM

An unforgettable part of Cubs lore, first baseman Leon Durham, a muscular left-handed hitter nicknamed "Bull," spent eight of his 10 years in the majors with Chicago.

A .277 career hitter, the six-foot, two-inch, 210-pound slugger regrettably is best remembered for allowing a ground ball go through his legs in the final game of the 1984 National League Championship Series against San Diego.

The '84 Cubs had a 3-0 lead with Cy Young Award winner Rick Sutcliffe on the mound. But the Padres scored two in the sixth and four runs in the seventh to grab their first pennant and seal the Cubs' collapse.

Even though he had a .991 career fielding percentage, many Cubs fans still blame Durham for the series loss in San Diego.

"The media talks about the 'Billy Goat Curse' and errors and situations that caused the Cubs not to go further...if they would just try to forget about the past and think about what's going on now, maybe things could turn over for the Cubs. Let's live now and forget about the past," says Durham, who has been the hitting coach for the Toledo Mud Hens in the Detroit Tigers' minor league system for over 15 years.

"Maybe I can get someone to give me an opportunity at the major league level pretty soon," said Durham in 2004.

Brace Photo

10 · LEON DURHAM · 1B
Years with Cubs: 1981-88

Two-time All-Star • Third leading hitter in NL in 1982 with .312 average • Hit 27 HR in 1987 and had 96 RBI in 1984 • Hit two HR in 1984 NLCS • Totaled 138 HR and 485 RBI with Cubs

Durham says it is true that one of his teammates accidentally knocked over a bucket of Gatorade on his first baseman's mitt in the dugout before he committed that fateful error in the '84 playoffs.

"I don't know who did it, but I had been on base," Durham said of the sticky predicament. "I think it happened as we were going back on the field. When you've got your sweetie pie, real glove with you, you don't trust another one. So I didn't feel like using my backup glove after the other one was soaked with Gatorade. So I stayed with it. The Gatorade and the error...it just went that way. It wasn't meant to happen for the Chicago Cubs."

Born July 31, 1957, in Cincinnati, Ohio, Durham was a first-round pick (15th overall) of the St. Louis Cardinals in the 1976 amateur draft. A graduate of Woodward High School in Cincinnati, Durham lettered for three years in baseball, football and basketball. He batted .365 with 16 home runs as a senior and went 11-3 as a pitcher and was named a high school All-American.

In 1979 he was named the American Association's Rookie of the Year after hitting .310 with 23 homers at Springfield. He drove in 88 runs in 127 games and stole 16 bases. Durham hit five homers and drove in 23 runs in 32 games for Springfield before his recall by the Cardinals. Durham's first major league homer came against the Cubs and pitcher Lynn McGlothlen on June 29, 1980 at Wrigley Field.

On December 9, 1980, Durham was traded by the Cardinals with a player to be named later and Ken Reitz to the Cubs for Bruce Sutter. St. Louis would later send Ty Waller to the Cubs to complete the trade. Durham hit .290 in 1981, his first season with the Cubs, leading the team with 25 stolen bases and six triples. He tied for the club lead with 10 home runs.

Durham's stint with the Cubs would end May 19, 1988, when he was traded to the Cincinnati Reds for Pat Perry and cash. He was released by the Reds November 8, 1988. He returned to the Cardinals on February 15, 1989 as a free agent.

Durham lost an arbitration case with the Cubs in 1985.

Arbitrator Steve Goldberg ruled the team had won its case against Durham, who had asked for a $1.1 million salary in 1985. He was instead paid what the team offered, $800,000.

"The Cubs emphasized in all their arguments that Leon was hurt in 1983 and missed a good part of the season, and that he was also on the disabled list [in '84]," said Richard Moss, Durham's agent.

"They said, in essence, that the injuries were the crucial factor, and the arbitrator apparently felt it was."

"I'm not bitter at anybody," Durham said at the Cubs' 1985 spring training in Mesa, Arizona. "You can say that I'm a happy Bull. I want to be treated with class and I'm going to show class now.

"We knew going into it that it was a no-lose situation. I really don't feel like a loser. I can remember when I made only $17,000 a year playing baseball. It's still an honor to be paid that kind of money [$800,000] and be considered in that class of ballplayers."

Durham was paid $983,333 by the Cubs in 1986, then $1,183,333 in 1987, and $1,383,333 in his final season with the Cubs in 1988.

Three different injuries in 1983 and a jammed shoulder in 1984 allowed Durham to play 237 of a possible 323 games.

"We argued that he wasn't as fragile a player as they made him out to be," Moss said. "Some of the things the Cubs' lawyers argued about were a little out of line."

Moss refused to identify particulars, but one of the things the Cubs emphasized was Durham's fielding, including the error that became critical to the Cubs' downfall in Game 5 of the National League playoffs.

"The biggest negative thing that the Cubs kept bringing up in the hearing was the injury thing," Durham said. "But that's okay. We were expecting that. The lowest blow that the Cubs kept bringing up was that fifth game of the playoffs in San Diego. They tried to lay all that on me, like I was the whole cause for us losing. I didn't think that was right. That was kind of dirty."

In 1984, Durham hit 19 of his 23 homers and drove in 61 of his 96 runs at home, batting .327 at Wrigley Field and .228 on the road. In 1983, he had nine homers, 38 RBIs and a .271 average at home; three homers, 17 RBIs and a .244 average on the road.

Only in 1982, Durham's best overall year in the majors, was he better on the road (13 HRs, 49 RBIs, .331) than at Wrigley Field (nine HRs, 41 RBIs, .296). His career numbers in his first four seasons as a Cub were: Home—.307 average, 45 homers, 169 RBIs; road—.265, 22 homers, 108 RBIs.

"Chills actually went through my body when I learned I had been named to the National League All-Star team," Durham said in 1982. That '82 Cubs team finished in fifth place with a 73-89 record, drawing 1,249,278 fans to Wrigley Field.

Durham was playing left field in those days as veteran Bill Buckner patrolled first base.

Buckner, rumored to be on the trading block all spring of '84, was sent to the bench and used sparingly as a pinch hitter because Durham had been shifted to first from the outfield. Buckner, understandably unhappy with his part-time status, was eventually traded for Dennis Eckersley.

After coming so close to a World Series appearance in 1984, Durham was struck by the irony of seeing the Cubs come within five outs of a World Series appearance in 2003.

"The Cubs were five outs from a World Series and had the error by the shortstop [Alex Gonzalez] and they had their ace [Mark Prior] throwing," said Durham. "Somebody is always going to be blamed no matter what."

Durham was hoping that the same injury bug that plagued the 1985 Cubs would not revisit the 2004 Cubs.

"In '85, there was nothing but injuries for everybody. I know that we had a chance to continue what we were doing in '84, but our starting five [pitchers] went down and we lost some other players," he said. "It was a disaster. Rick Sutcliffe [hamstring] was one of the first ones to go down. Then it was Scott Sanderson and Dick Ruthven. Dennis Eckersley even had the bad hamstring at one point. And [closer] Lee Smith's thumb was bothering him. So now this year [2004] we have Mark Prior starting out with a bad Achilles. But the Cubs have better pitching depth now with Kerry Wood, Greg Maddux and Matt Clement than we did back then."

Durham was an accomplished hitter and fielder who continues to hope his name will not forever be linked to the Cubs' postseason futility.

Where Have You Gone?

DENNIS ECKERSLEY

Dennis Eckersley is yet another former Cubs players who would become a Hall of Famer based on his performances with another club.

Eckersley, who was selected for enshrinement in 2004 by the Baseball Writers Association of America, was a member of the Cubs from 1984-86 before being dealt to Oakland for three minor leaguers who never made it in the big leagues.

"My confidence was low when I was traded by the Cubs. I had to make some changes in my personal life, as well," said Eckersley, who went through substance abuse rehabilitation to straighten out his life.

Former Cubs general manager Dallas Green acquired Eckersley and minor league infielder Mike Brumley from Boston on May 25, 1984.

Eckersley was 10-8 with a 3.03 earned run average with the Cubs in '84, and lost a 7-1 decision to the San Diego Padres in Game 3 of the NLCS. He was 11-7 in '85 and 6-11 in '86.

Eckersley and minor league infielder Dan Rohn were traded from the Cubs to Oakland on April 3, 1987, for three minor leaguers. On April 12, 1975, Eckersley made his debut in relief against the Brewers in Milwaukee. His first strikeout victim was Robin Yount.

Brace Photo

40/43 · DENNIS ECKERSLEY · P
Years with Cubs: 1984-86

Went 10-8 with 3.03 ERA in 1984 and 11-7 with 3.08 ERA in 1985 •
Started one game in 1984 NLCS • Won 27 games in 81 starts with Cubs
• Elected to Baseball Hall of Fame

Eckersley, 58, was a starter and a reliever for 24 seasons. He broke in with the Cleveland Indians, where he tossed a no-hitter in 1977. Eckersley won 151 games before becoming a full-time reliever.

"All I had to do was pitch one or two innings, so I could be the type of pitcher I was when I was 20 years old," said Eckersley. "I could challenge people and throw strikes. I always had pretty good control."

In 1978 he was 20-8 and completed 16 games for the Red Sox. In his rookie season he won 13 games and had an impressive 2.60 ERA. In 1976 he struck out 200 batters. His career record as a starter included a 3.71 ERA and 1,609 strikeouts.

Eckersley credits former Oakland manager Tony LaRussa and pitching coach Dave Duncan for resurrecting his career.

"I think Duncan had the foresight to see what I could do. And I think Tony had confidence in me," said Eckersley. "I think that played a huge part in my success."

Eckersley twice led the AL in saves and ended his career as the league's record holder for career saves with 324. He won the MVP and Cy Young Awards in 1992, his best season in the big leagues. He produced one of the best seasons ever by a closer in '92 as he led the A's to the playoffs. In 69 games he saved 51, won seven, posted a 1.91 ERA and fanned 93 in 80 innings. He walked just 11 batters, giving him 27 walks in his last 287 regular season innings.

Eckersley was only the third reliever (Hoyt Wilhelm and Rollie Fingers are the others) to be elected to the Hall of Fame. He was part of the Hall of Fame class that included infielder Paul Molitor, broadcaster Lon Simmons and baseball writer Murray Chass.

Eckersley always was cool, calm and collected when he was on the mound. When he delivered his Hall of Fame acceptance speech in 2004, he showed more emotion as he reminisced about his childhood baseball memories.

"You know, I wanted to pitch like [Juan] Marichal and hit like Willie Mays," he said. "You know, we didn't go to many Giant games, but when I did, I savored every moment. I couldn't take my eyes off Willie Mays. I was fascinated by that basket catch. I tried to emulate Marichal's high leg kick. And that's where the dream began."

Eckersley talked about how he was able to hone his pitching skills as a youngster by playing ball with his older brother, Wally, and his older friends.

Among the many people he thanked, Eckersley singled out his high school coach Bill Lightfoot for his support. He also mentioned two high school buddies who would become lifelong friends: Mike Jacinto and Jeff Pimental.

And, of course, Eckersley thanked his parents as he showed even more emotion.

He began his career as a starter, and it wasn't until he was 32 years old and playing for LaRussa that he became a closer. He went on to save 320 games for the Oakland A's in nine seasons, helping the team to four division titles, three pennants, and a World Series title. He retired as the No. 3 all-time saves leader.

Nicknamed "Eck," the sidewinding right-hander played for the Cleveland Indians (1975-1977), Boston Red Sox (1978-1984, 1998), Chicago Cubs (1984-1986), Oakland A's (1987-1995) and St. Louis Cardinals (1996-1997).

His postseason participation included: 1984 National League Championship Series, 1988 American League Championship Series, 1988 World Series, 1989 ALCS, 1989 World Series, 1990 ALCS, 1990 World Series, 1992 ALCS, 1996 NLDS, 1996 NLCS, 1998 ALDS.

Eckersley started and lost Game 3 of the '84 NLCS with the Cubs. In the 1988, 1989 and 1990 ALCSs Eck pitched in 11 of the A's 13 games, with a 0.60 ERA and nine saves. His 11 saves in LCS play are a major league record record. He helped Oakland win the 1989 World Series.

He was also a six-time All-Star: 1977, 1982, 1988, 1990-1992. Then came the American League MVP 1992, AL Cy Young 1992, Rolaids Relief Man 1988, 1992 and 1988 ALCS MVP.

Eckersley was drafted by the Cleveland Indians in the third round of the 1972 amateur draft on June 6, 1972. On March 30, 1978, he was traded by the Indians with Fred Kendall to the Boston Red Sox for Rick Wise, Mike Paxton, Ted Cox, and Bo Diaz.

On May 25, 1984, he was dealt by the Red Sox with Mike Brumley to the Cubs for Buckner. He was granted free agency on November 8, 1984 and re-signed as a free agent with the Cubs. Then on April 3, 1987, he was traded by the Cubs with Dan Rohn to the Oakland Athletics for Brian Guinn (minors), Dave Wilder (minors), and Mark Leonette (minors).

On October 25, 1994, he was granted free agency and signed on April 3, 1995, with Oakland. He was traded by Oakland to the St. Louis Cardinals for Steve Montgomery on February 13, 1996. He again became a free agent on October 29, 1997, and signed with the Red Sox.

On May 30, 1977, Eckersley hurled a no-hitter against the Angels, striking out 12 batters. On September 3, 1988, he set an AL record with his 37th save of the season. On September 26, 1998, he set a major league record by appearing in his 1,071st game, breaking Wilhelm's mark. It was his final game.

At age 43, Eckersley walked just 113 batters in 779 2/3 innings (1.3 per nine innings pitched).

LEE ELIA

An inauspicious major league playing career included brief stints as an infielder in 1966 and 1968 with the Chicago Cubs and the Chicago White Sox. But Lee Elia will forever be remembered for his profanity-laced tirade when he was the manager of the Cubs two decades later.

On April, 29, 1983, Elia lost all his composure during a postgame press conference. The Cubs started the season with a 5-14 record and had just lost to the Pittsburgh Pirates in front of a small crowd at Wrigley Field that registered its disapproval with boos.

Here is the sanitized, PG-rated transcript of his outburst:

"[Bleep] those [bleepin'] fans who come out here and say they're Cub fans that are supposed to be behind you, rippin' every [bleeping] thing you do. I'll tell you one [bleeping] thing, I hope we get [bleeping] hotter than [bleep], just to stuff it up them 3,000 (bleeping) people that show up every [bleeping] day, because if they're the real Chicago [bleeping] fans, they can kiss my [bleeping] ass right downtown, and print it!

"They're really, really behind you around here... my [bleeping] ass. What the [bleep] am I supposed to do, go out there and let my [bleeping] players get destroyed every day and be quiet about it? For the [bleeping] nickel-dime people who turn up? The [bleepers] don't even work. That's why they're out at the [bleeping] game. They oughta go out and

Brace Photo

19/4 (MANAGER) · LEE ELIA · IF
Years with Cubs: 1968 (player), 1982-83 (manager)

Played 15 games during 1968 season with Cubs • Won 127 games as Cubs manager

get a [bleeping] job and find out what it's like to go out and earn a [bleeping] living. Eighty-five percent of the [bleeping] world is working. The other fifteen percent come out here. A [bleeping] playground for the [bleepers]. Rip them [bleepers]. Rip them [bleeping] [bleepers] like the [bleeping] players. We got guys bustin' their [bleeping] ass, and them [bleeping] people boo. And that's the Cubs? My players get around here. I haven't seen it this [bleeping] year. Everybody associated with this organization have been winners their whole [bleeping] life. Everybody. And the credit is not given in that respect.

"All right, they don't show because we're five and 14... and unfortunately, that's the criteria of them dumb 15 [bleeping] percent that come out to day baseball. The other 85 percent are earning a living. I tell you, it'll take more than a five and 12 or five and 14 to destroy the makeup of this club. I guarantee you that. There's some [bleeping] pros out there that wanna win. But you're stuck in a [bleeping] stigma of the [bleeping] Dodgers and the Phillies and the Cardinals and all that cheap [bleep]. It's unbelievable. It really is. It's a disheartening [bleeping] situation that we're in right now. Anybody who was associated with the Cub organization four or five years ago that came back and sees the multitude of progress that's been made will understand that if they're baseball people, that five and 14 doesn't negate all that work. We got 143 [bleeping] games left.

"What I'm tryin' to say is don't rip them [bleeping] guys out there. Rip me. If you wanna rip somebody, rip my [bleeping] ass. But don't rip them [bleeping] guys 'cause they're givin' everything they can give. And right now they're tryin' to do more than God gave 'em, and that's why we make the simple mistakes. That's exactly why."

It took many years for Elia to come to grips with the fact that his 1983 post-game outburst would forever become part of baseball lore. Whenever other coaches in any sport would lose control of their emotions after a game, Elia's legendary tirade immediately would be referenced as the standard bearer.

It wasn't until the 25-year anniversary of Elia's profane monologue that he began marketing a book and tape of the legendary outburst. Elia traveled to Chicago and appeared on various radio and television programs, appearing to have a little fun with the renewed notoriety. At long last Elia admitted that he had "lost it" after that game and had enough of the criticism from fans and media.

During the 2008 season, Elia was employed by the Seattle Mariners and held three different coaching assignments. First, he was named special assistant to the manager, by John McLaren. Then he was moved into the position of hitting coach on June 9, 2008, when Jeff Pentland was dismissed. Just a couple of weeks after that, he was promoted to bench coach when McLaren was fired as manager. When Elia was fired by the Mariners after the 2008 season, the Dodgers hired him as a special assistant to General Manager Ned Colletti.

Elia and Colletti had a long-time relationship dating back to their days working with the Cubs.

For a man who devoted his entire life to baseball as a player, manager, coach and management consultant, it is unfortunate that Elia's name should be associated strictly to that dreary afternoon at Wrigley Field in 1983.

As a player, Elia hit .205 in 80 games with the White Sox in 1966. As a member of the Cubs in '68, Elia hit .176 in 15 games.

Born July 16, 1937, in Philadelphia, Pennsylvania, Lee Constantine Elia was signed as an amateur free agent in 1959 by the Phillies. On December 1, 1964, he was traded along with Danny Cater to the White Sox for pitchers Ray Herbert and Jeoff Long.

On May 23, 1967, Elia's contract was purchased by the Cubs. And on April 19, 1969, Elia was traded to the New York Yankees for Nate Colbert.

Elia has held several coaching jobs. In 2002, he was hired as Special Assistant to Player Development of the Alanta Braves.

Longtime friend Dallas Green credits Elia with developing Lee Smith into the game's all-time saves leader. When Elia was the manager of the Cubs, he saw that Smith was better equipped to come out of the bullpen than serve as a starter.

"Lee Smith was one of my favorite people," said Green. "He was one of the few Cub guys we could count on when we got there from Philadelphia [in 1981]. Lee Elia gets credit for making him a relief pitcher and should get a lot of credit for Mr. Smith going into the Hall of Fame."

Elia guided the Cubs to a 73-89 record in 1982 as the team finished in fifth place. Elia was fired as manager of the Cubs in August of 1983 and replaced on an interim basis by Charlie Fox. The Cubs were 54-69 when Elia was fired. The team had been just three and a half games out of first place at the All-Star break.

In 1984, Jim Frey took over as Cubs manager and led them to a surprise first-place finish in the NL East. Two years later, Frey was fired as Cubs manager.

Green felt Elia and Frey could have been more successful if the organization had made a greater and quicker commitment to win. Green was relieved of his duties as Cubs president and general manager in 1988.

"There is no question," Green says now. "We were not prepared to win [a World Series] in 1984. I have never been big on timetables. I didn't come in from Philadelphia with any five-year plans or anything like that. I wanted to make it successful as quickly as we could, and fortunately we did. Gordon Goldsberry did a tremendous job in totally revamping the scouting and development program. Unfortunately for him and for me, none of our fruits came to bear until we left. Most of our time there we had to make do with trades and free agency. It wasn't until we left that Greg Maddux and Rafael Palmeiro and Mark Grace and Shawon Dunston and all those kids started to produce."

Elia received another opportunity to manage in the middle of the 1987 season with the Phillies. He had a 51-50 record with them that season, but slipped to 60-92 in 1988, when Philadelphia wound up in sixth place. His career managerial record was 238-300 for a .442 winning percentage.

MARK GRACE

One of the most astute pure hitters in Cubs history, first baseman Mark Grace carved his indelible niche as a productive and popular ballplayer throughout his long career.

"He always came to play," said center fielder Steve Finley, one of Grace's teammates with Arizona. "He came to play, and he came to have fun. He knew how to do both at the same time."

Grace wound up his playing career in the Valley of the Sun in 2003 after finally earning a World Series ring with the D-Backs in 2001.

The 6-foot, two-inch, 190-pound Grace married Tanya Avila in January, 2002. The couple divorced in 2006. They have two sons—Jackson Gene and Preston Torre.

Grace had been handling color commentary for Arizona Diamondbacks games when he was relieved of his duties in October, 2012, after being arrested a third time for drunk driving. On Oct. 3, 2012 Grace was indicted on four felony counts based on his Aug. 23, 2012, arrest for suspicion of driving under the influence, driving with a suspended license and without an interlock device.

Mark Eugene Grace was born June 28, 1964, in Winston-Salem, North Carolina, to parents Gene and Sharon Grace. The family moved 13 times in 25 years, truly testing Mark's ability to make friends and

Tom Hauck/Getty Images

17 · MARK GRACE · 1B
Years with Cubs: 1988-2000

Three-time All-Star • Four-time NL Gold Glove Award • Led NL with 51 doubles in 1995 • Hit .300 nine times • Had .998 fielding percentage in 1992 • Batted .647 with one HR and eight RBI in 1989 NLCS • Played in 1998 NLDS • Totaled 148 HR and 1,004 RBI with Cubs

adapt on the fly. One of the family's many stops was St. Louis, where Grace avidly began to follow the career of former Cardinals first baseman Keith Hernandez.

Grace could relate to Hernandez, who was a slick fielder and a high-average hitter with limited power. Both are left-handed. Grace later would be compared to Hernandez because of his remarkably similar skills.

Grace spent most of his teenage years in southern California, where he attended Tustin High School near Los Angeles. He was a member of both the baseball and basketball teams, and even took time to be a member of the prom court during his senior year.

His first stop out of high school was not to the big leagues, but to Saddleback Junior College.

Selected by the Minnesota Twins in the 15th round of the 1984 January draft, Grace opted not to sign. Later drafted by the Cubs in the 24th round of the amateur draft on June 3, 1985, and then signed, Grace's chances of making the quantum leap to the big leagues did not appear overwhelming at first.

But his 16 seasons in the major leagues would end with an imposing .303 career batting average. Grace collected more hits (1,754) in the 1990s than any other player in the National League. He had a lifetime .329 batting average in the playoffs. A four-time Gold Glove fielder and three-time NL All-Star, the only aspect of Grace's game that likely will keep him out of the Hall of Fame is the fact he lacked great power for a first baseman, a traditional home run hitting position.

"Back in 1990 or '91, [former Cubs managers] Jim Frey and Don Zimmer told me they wanted me to get on top of some pitches and jerk some balls out of the ballpark," Grace said. "But by the All-Star break I was hitting .260 with three home runs. And Zim came up to me and said: 'Kid, you tried it and you did what we told you. But when you tried it, it didn't work. Go back to your way.'

"And by the end of the season, I was hitting .309 with nine home runs. So I still feel my way is the right way for me."

While Grace did not produce prodigious home run numbers, the Cubs of the 1980s and '90s got home runs from nontraditional positions such as second base. Ryne Sandberg wound up his career with more homers than any other second baseman in big league history.

"I don't think it matters where you get it from. If you have three or four guys who can hit it out of the ballpark, it doesn't matter," said Grace during the height of his career in Chicago. "Even though I am not a home run hitter, I don't consider myself a singles hitter either."

Grace clubbed 511 doubles during his career, compared to 173 home runs.

"That means, when a guy is on first base, he is possibly in scoring position for me. I feel that I am a quality hitter. Yeah, I don't hit a heck of a lot of home runs. But that doesn't bother me at all. I will be out there on base for Sammy [Sosa] though, I can tell you that much."

Jim Riggleman managed Grace and the Cubs when they faced the Atlanta Braves in the 1998 National League Championship Series.

"After having such a rough season in 1997, the 1998 season was special," said Riggleman. "The things Sammy Sosa did, challenging Roger Maris's home run record with Mark McGwire...that and our getting into the playoffs certainly were the highlights. There were a lot of great memories about managing the ball club. It kind of got lost in the shuffle that year that Mark Grace had more doubles [364] than anyone else in the decade of the '90s. There was such emphasis on the home run during that time."

On May 12, 1998, as a member of the Cubs, Grace became the first player to hit a home run into the Bank One Ballpark pool beyond the right center field wall. On July 29, 1998, Grace became the first visiting player to hit a second home run into the pool.

Named to the Cubs' All-Century Team by the fans in 1999, Grace batted .647 in the 1989 NLCS against the Giants.

Known for his sense of humor and good nature, Grace never missed an opportunity to play a practical joke or take a fun jab at a teammate. And he was never above self-deprecating humor, either.

When the Diamondbacks were being blown out in a game on September 2, 2002, Grace was summoned to make his first and only major league relief pitching appearance. Grace gave up a home run to rookie David Ross during his stint as the Dodgers whipped the D-Backs 19-1.

"I didn't have a scouting report on him," Grace quipped. "Obviously he can hit 65-mile-per-hour fastballs."

Immediately after winning the World Series in 2001, Grace said: "If you only understood how great this is for me. It was better than anything I could have imagined. It is better than sex. But then again, I'm kind of lousy at that."

Grace and former Cubs Cy Young Award winner Rick Sutcliffe stayed friends. Sutcliffe now handles baseball broadcast duties on ESPN. Grace provided color commentary for ESPN Radio during the 1999 and 2000 postseasons.

"One day when I was with the Cubs, we were in Cincy, where they'd set off fireworks after a home run, and [Sutcliffe] gives up back-to-back home runs," Grace recalled after his retirement. "So there's fireworks going off all over the place, Sut's [ticked] off, and here comes our pitching coach, Billy Connors. Well, like I said, Sut's [ticked] already, so as soon as he sees Billy he says, 'Get your fat [butt] back in the dugout. I know what I'm doing out here. And tell [manager Don] Zimmer to settle down, too.' But Billy keeps coming, and when he gets there he says, very calmly, 'I know you know what you're doing. I'm just giving the guy who sets the fireworks off time to reload.'"

Regarding former Cubs shortstop Shawon Dunston, Grace quipped: "I owe him a lot. Nobody would know how good I was at digging balls out of the dirt if it wasn't for him and all those bad throws."

Rumors and reports surfaced during the '90s that Grace and slugging star Sammy Sosa did not get along personally and that professional jealousy may have divided the Cubs' locker room. Grace tried to dispel those notions when the two were teammates. But after he joined the Diamondbacks, Grace could not help but poke fun at Sosa when he was caught using a corked bat in 2003.

"Had I known when I played in Chicago there were corked bats in the bat rack, I probably would have hit 25 home runs," Grace cracked. "[Sosa] is going to have to answer a lot of questions. It's weird. Instead of hitting them 500 feet, he wants to hit them 550, I guess."

Grace was eligible for free agency in 1994 and was re-signed by the Cubs on April 7, 1995. After being paid $140,000 to play for the Cubs in 1989, his salary jumped to $4.4 million in 1995. Grace signed as a free agent with the Diamondbacks on December 8, 2000, for $3 million, after being paid $5.3 million by the Cubs the year before.

Grace left the Cubs kicking and screaming, as angry words were expressed through his longtime agent Barry Axelrod toward Cubs president Andy MacPhail.

When the Diamondbacks won the World Series the next season, Grace took that opportunity to heap more words of disdain on the Cubs organization for failing to offer him a comparable contract.

One of the biggest hits of his career came in Game 7 of the 2001 World Series against the Yankees. His single ignited a rally that teammate Luis Gonzalez capped with a game-winning single.

"I knew I had to get on base for anything to happen," said Grace, who was even willing to be hit by a pitch to climb aboard. "I thought to myself, a concussion heals in 30 days, right?"

The 2003 season was a long one for Grace, who was used sparingly. He had a .189 average in just 64 games. With the Cubs he had hit over .300 in nine of 11 years at one point. When he retired, Grace was 93rd on the all-time hit list with 2,443, three shy of Dwight Evans.

RICHIE HEBNER

Known as "Hacker" because of his free-swinging style at the plate, Richie Hebner spent 18 seasons in the big leagues, the final two with the Cubs in 1984 and '85.

"Chicago is the greatest city in the world," said Hebner, who began as the manager of the North Shore Navigators in 2012. "During the two years that I played for the Cubs, I kept asking everybody, 'Does anybody work in this town? Everybody is at the games.' It was a fun place to play."

Hebner has coached in several organizations at the Major and Minor League levels since retiring as a player.

Originally a first-round draft choice of the Pirates in 1966, Hebner played with Pittsburgh, Philadelphia, New York (NL), Detroit and Chicago. In 1,908 career games, he batted .276 with 203 home runs and 890 RBIs.

Born November 26, 1947, in Norwood, Massachusetts, Richard Joseph Hebner hit .301 in his first full season of 1969 to lead NL rookies. His Pirate teammates then included Roberto Clemente, Willie Stargell, Bill Mazeroski, Manny Sanguillen, Gene Garber and Al Oliver.

Hebner was a multitalented athlete at Norwood Senior High School, where he lettered for four years in baseball and hockey. He won scholastic All-America honors in hockey and was offered a contract by

Brace Photo

18 · RICHIE HEBNER · 1B/3B
Years with Cubs: 1984-85

Batted .333 in 1984 • Played in 1984 NLCS • Totaled five HR and 30 RBI in 127 games with Cubs

the Boston Bruins. National Hockey League scout Gary Eggleston thought Hebner was the best New England hockey player he ever saw coming out of high school.

His first minor league stint was with the Salem Rebels of the Appalachian League, where Hebner batted .359 in 26 games. In his second pro season, he played for Raleigh, North Carloina, of the Carolina (A) League and hit .336 in 78 games.

On October 5, 1971, Hebner's home run off San Francisco's Juan Marichal in the eigth inning gave the Pirates a 2-1 victory and a 2-1 lead in the National League Championship Series.

The next day, Pittsburgh thumped the Giants 9-5 to win the series three games to one and take the Pirates into the World Series. Hebner had three hits—including a home run—and three RBIs in the clincher.

Hebner, who played third base and first base during his career, swatted a career-high 25 home runs in 1973.

When his former Pirates teammate Willie Stargell passed away in 2001, Hebner referred to the Hall of Fame first baseman as one of his best teammates ever.

"Late in my career—I had maybe 12-13 years in the majors—I returned to the Pirates and hit a pinch-hit grand slam off Lee Smith," Hebner was quoted as saying in *USA Today*. "Willie walked up to me in the clubhouse and gave me a star, something he did for his teammates. I'd been around forever, but it gave me goose bumps. Imagine how a young player felt after getting a star from Pops."

Hebner batted left and threw right and was used extensively as a pinch hitter in his latter years.

His father, Bill, was a foreman at a cemetery, and Hebner worked as a grave digger during the off season. He signed originally with the Pirates for $40,000 and missed some time early in his career to serve in the military reserves.

A member of five division championship teams with the Pirates over seven seasons as a third baseman, Hebner then spent two seasons at first base helping the Phillies win NL East titles in 1977 and 1978.

Free agent Pete Rose supplanted him in 1979, so Hebner moved on to the Mets and drove in 79 runs that season. The Phillies had traded Hebner and second baseman Jose Moreno to the Mets for pitcher Nino Espinosa.

Hebner was traded to the Tigers on October 31, 1979, for third baseman Phil Mankowski and outfielder Jerry Morales. Hebner then had a career-high 82 RBIs in 1980 in just 104 games (341 at-bats). After a second stint with Pittsburgh, he became the No. 1 pinch hitter for the

1984 Cubs, who won the NL East that season.

On August 16, 1982, Hebner returned to the Pirates. And on September 14 of that season, Hebner and Bill Madlock each hit grand slams to lead the Pirates to a 15-5 rout of the Cubs.

An excellent natural hitter, Hebner once said this about trying to hit Phil Niekro's vaunted knuckleball: "Hitting Niekro's knuckleball is like eating soup with a fork."

The Cubs acquired Hebner on January 5, 1984, so his wife, Patricia, and daughters, Elizabeth and Katherine, saw him join his fourth big league club.

"I went back to the Cubs Fan Convention last January. It was a lot of fun," said Hebner in 2004. "A lot of the guys from the '84 team showed up."

Hebner hit .333 with a career-high .407 on-base percentage as a pinch hitter for the Cubs. He was 27 for 81 as a pinch hitter, including several clutch hits.

The Cubs ended 39 years of frustration by clinching the National League East title in Pittsburgh on September 24, 1984. A cozy crowd of only 5,472 was on hand for this historic event at Three Rivers Stadium.

Rick Sutcliffe caught the corner on the Pirates' Joe Orsulak for a called third strike. The Cubs captured the division title behind Sutcliffe's masterful two-hitter. Sutcliffe struck out nine and walked none as the Cubs defeated the Pirates 4-1.

"Last year the Cubs couldn't beat the Hilton Hotel cooks. A few trades later, we're champs," Hebner exclaimed then.

The Cubs' 1984 regular season defied all odds. They were a team that had finished fifth the previous season with a 71-91 mark. The Cubs had lost 11 straight exhibition games in the spring of '84 and finished with the worst exhibition record in all of baseball. Then they suddenly ruled their division with a 96-65 record—a turnaround of 25 games.

Hebner was sidelined much of the second half of the '84 season with biceptal tendinitis in his right shoulder. But he contributed several key hits early in the season. He hit a game-winning home run in the ninth inning off Bruce Sutter in St. Louis on April 24, 1984.

"It's funny how you get a lot of letters from fans," Hebner said during the '84 season as he tried to play through his shoulder pain. "At least they care and know you're still breathing. But the remedies seldom work."

He swatted his 200th career homer off San Francisco's Greg Minton in a pinch-hit role on May 8, 1984. Hebner was hitless in one at-bat during the National League Championship Series against San Diego that postseason.

Hebner loved the atmosphere in and around Wrigley Field, as well as the quaintness of the ballpark. In 1973, Hebner said: "I stand at the plate in Philadelphia and I honestly don't know whether I'm in Pittsburgh, Cincinnati, St. Louis or Philly. They all look alike."

In 1985, Hebner tied for the Major League lead in pinch-hit RBIs with 12. He shared the honor with Terry Whitfield of the Dodgers. Hebner was hitting.324 as a pinch hitter on August 14 with 12 hits in 37 at-bats. He homered against Montreal on that date. But he failed to get a hit in his final 22 pinch hit appearances the remainder of the '84 season. He wound up hitting just .203 (12 for 59) overall as a pinch hitter.

The Cubs wound up finishing 23 1/2 games out of first place in 1985 because of numerous injuries.

"There's been more noise in my father's graveyard than there's been at Wrigley Field the last few days," Hebner quipped during that disappointing season.

Former Cubs general manager Dallas Green was busy during the winter meetings in San Diego following the '85 season. He acquired switch-hitting outfielder Jerry Mumphrey in exchange for promising young outfielder Billy Hatcher in a deal with Houston. Green also picked up veteran second baseman Manny Trillo, a former Cub of the '70s, from the San Francisco Giants for utility infielder Dave Owen.

"Jerry and Manny really strengthen our bench," said Green. "If Jerry starts, whoever sits will make the bench that much stronger. When he doesn't start, Jerry will give us the versatility of a switch hitter on the bench."

The deals made Hebner more expendable.

Hebner was released by the Cubs April 1, 1986. He was not amused by the April Fool's Day transaction. But he managed to make light of it later.

"People don't know it, but Ted Williams and I had a lot in common," Hebner said. "We both hit home runs in our last major league at-bats. The only difference was he knew it was his last. I was released the next year."

KEN HOLTZMAN

An aggressive, control-conscious left-hander, Ken Holtzman enjoyed great postseason success, but not with the Chicago Cubs.

Holtzman pitched for the Cubs (1965-1971, 1978-1979), Oakland A's (1972-1975), Baltimore Orioles (1976) and New York Yankees (1976-1978).

In 13 postseason starts, Holtzman was 6-4 with a stingy 2.30 earned run average in more than 70 innings pitched.

Holtzman started Games 1, 4 and 7 of the 1973 World Series for Oakland against the New York Mets. He left Game 7 with a 5-1 lead in the sixth inning and got the win after relief help from Rollie Fingers and Darold Knowles.

Born November 3, 1945, in St. Louis, Kenneth Dale Holtzman made his major league debut September 4, 1965. The six-foot, two-inch, 175-pounder had a career record of 174-150 and a 3.49 earned run average.

Particularly adept at inducing ground-ball outs, Holtzman was involved in three major trades.

"The first time I was traded [to Oakland for outfielder Rick Monday] was under circumstances where I was frustrated that the Cubs didn't win," said Holtzman. "I felt at that time that the front office could

Brace Photo

30 · KEN HOLTZMAN · P
Years with Cubs: 1965-71, 1978-79

Went 9-0 in 12 starts in 1967 • Won 17 games in 1969 and 1970 •
Struck out 202 in 1970 • Totaled 80 wins and made 191 appearances
with Cubs

have done a little bit more to make it more conducive to winning. I was frustrated at the end of the '71 season and I told Mr. [John] Holland [former Cubs GM], 'Look, I am not interested in any individual-type awards or any of that kind of stuff. I want to win. I want to see what it is like to play in a World Series. And I just disagree with the philosophy around here.'

"I asked to be traded. So they traded me to Oakland. It was like I went to baseball heaven. And, obviously, we won all the time out there. Then I was traded from there to the Yankees and we won there. Obviously, I was very fortunate in my career. I was in a lot of World Series and on a lot of championship teams.

"After having experienced that, I think that I was right. Because those teams had one thing in common, that winning was more important than the welfare of the individual players. You like to be liked and you like to be friends. There is nothing wrong with that. But the ultimate goal of winning is even more important than being liked or being popular. There are hard decisions, and if it means cutting a guy, or going out and getting a guy at the end of the season…sometimes you have to do it."

Toward that end, Holtzman eventually came to respect flamboyant former Oakland owner Charlie Finley and demanding Yankees boss George Steinbrenner.

Holtzman joined starting pitchers Vida Blue, Catfish Hunter and Blue Moon Odom in Oakland and helped the A's to three straight World Series titles. Holtzman was 4-1 with a 2.54 ERA in eight World Series starts.

"I enjoyed my years with the Cubs, but I was able to win World Series rings with Oakland," said Holtzman in 2004. "I maintain contact with some of the former Cubs. In July we had a reunion in Oakland of the three-time world champion A's teams. Periodically they invite old broken-down players like me and we get to renew a lot of old acquaintances."

Holtzman tossed a 3-0 no-hitter against the Atlanta Braves on August 19, 1969, while with the Cubs. He pitched a second no-hitter for the Cubs, defeating the Cincinnati Reds 1-0, on June 3, 1971. Holtzman scored the only run of that game.

"Boy, the years are going by. My first no-hitter was in '69," said Holtzman in 2004. "That's 35 years ago. That was kind of a magical year in '69. People to this day think of 1969 as being a one-of-a-kind year. We were in first place for most of the year and everybody expected us to win. Yet we didn't. The no-hit game was right when we had our biggest lead. We must have been seven or eight games in first place. And there were 40,000 screaming fanatics at the ballpark. Standing room only every day. We couldn't even walk to our cars out in the parking lot.

"That particular day, the wind was blowing in and I got lucky. That's what they are—luck. I have often said that a no-hit game is a well pitched game with an added dose of luck. And that's what that was. The wind was blowing in. Hank Aaron hit a ball that would have been out normally, but the wind blew it back and we won 3-0.

"I remember not so much the pitch-by-pitch, but just the excitement that we were in first place. And then we went downhill from there."

Holtzman tossed a second no-hitter two years later.

"I wasn't having that good a year, particularly," said Holtzman. "I believe it was the second game of a doubleheader in Cincinnati. It was a hot, muggy night. It was just one of those things where I happened to have good stuff. And everything they hit was right at somebody."

Holtzman combined the knowledge imparted by Cubs pitching coaches and veteran colleagues to kick-start his impressive career.

"I can remember when Leo Durocher was hired [as Cubs manager]; he brought with him Freddy Fitzsimmons," said Holtzman. "Then, of course, we had Joe Becker. Those guys helped me a lot. They were in the game for a long time. Primarily, they were good strategic helpers. They helped you with how to pitch, not necessarily the mechanical part of the game. You need the mechanics, but also you need somebody who could get the big picture. I thought Joe was very good at that, and so was Freddy.

"But I learned more from Bill Hands and Fergie Jenkins—two fellow starting pitchers—even more than I did from any pitching coach."

Asked to name his most commanding pitch, Holtzman began to discuss his mound strategy.

"Whether it was a breaking ball or a fastball, I always felt that the best pitch a pitcher can throw is strike one," said Holtzman. "You might have a 98-mile-an-hour fastball or a 78-mile-an-hour fastball. But if you can get ahead of the batter, you can kind of work off any ability or talent you have to win the game. That is the ultimate aim.

"The ultimate aim is not about earned run average or strikeouts. That takes care of itself if you understand the strategy of pitching. Strike one is the most important pitch. I used to pride myself on getting ahead of the hitter. That made that entire sequence of facing that batter a lot easier.

"Now, I had a decent fastball. I wasn't a flamethrower. But I threw hard enough. I had an average or better than average breaking ball, which I only threw very rarely. I felt my prime quality was my control."

Holtzman's best season was 1973 when he won 21 games, pitched nearly 300 innings and also won two games in the World Series. In 1973, Holtzman allowed an average of just two walks per nine innings and had 16 complete games among his 40 starts. He was a key factor in Oakland's second straight World Series title.

Holtzman has fashioned quite a different career since retiring from baseball.

"I am the health and physical education supervisor for the St. Louis Jewish Community Center," said Holtzman in 2004. "We're located about 30 miles west of the city of St. Louis in a suburb called Chesterfield, Missouri ... We have a beautiful facility. Gyms, batting cages, fields, five swimming pools, tennis courts. And we run year-round for kids through adults.

"It's totally different [from playing major league baseball]," said Holtzman in 2004. "I have been retired now for 24 years from baseball. I was in business in Chicago before I moved back to St. Louis. Then I got into teaching, and teaching led me to this. That is what I have been doing ever since. It is a lot of fun every single day. This is an offshoot of teaching where I not only get to teach, but also coach, organize and be an administrator. I kind of enjoy the variety."

Despite his philosophical differences with the Cubs' front office, Holtzman said he will always have special feelings for the Cubs.

"That's where I started, with the Cubs," he said. "I went to the University of Illinois and I was drafted by the Cubs in the first free agent draft. And I still maintain to this day that my biggest thrill was walking onto the field at Wrigley Field for the first time in 1965. That's still my biggest thrill.

"In fact, the first person who picked me up at the airport was Buck O'Neil, who had been a Negro League player and worked for the Cubs as a scout. He took me to the park, and that's where I met Ernie Banks and Ron Santo and Billy Williams and all the guys. I still think that was my biggest thrill, even with all the World Series and All-Star games I played in later in my career."

"In 1965 and '66, I was probably the youngest guy on the Cubs' staff, by far. They had Larry Jackson and Ernie Broglio, Dick Ellsworth and Bob Buhl and all these old guys who were in their thirties and had spent many years in the major leagues," said Holtzman. "They were kind of on the downside of their career. And we finished last all the time.

"In '66, that's when they traded for Fergie and Bill Hands, and they got Randy Hundley and Don Kessinger and Glenn Beckert and all the guys started coming up together," said Holtzman. "In '67, it was the first year the Cubs had finished in the first division in over 20 years. Then for the next five or six years, even though we didn't win it, the Cubs had a pretty good nucleus."

Holtzman can't help but notice the way the finances of the game have affected the way players are treated these days.

"In those days when I played, one of the things I remember is that if you were a starting pitcher, on your middle days, you would be asked to pitch in relief," said Holtzman in 2004. "I remember Fergie Jenkins and I would come in to relieve. If a manager needed you to pitch to a hitter or two, you went in to relieve. I can remember two days after I pitched my no-hitter in Cincinnati, I was in the bullpen in Atlanta. I guess the game has changed, right?"

Where Have You Gone?

BURT HOOTON

Drafted by the Cubs in the first round (second pick) of the 1971 amateur draft, Burt Hooton gained his greatest notoriety by pitching a no-hitter against the Philadelphia Phillies in just his fourth major league game.

Burt Carlton Hooton, who was born February 7, 1950, in Greenville, Texas, had a 151-136 record over 15 major league seasons with the Cubs, Dodgers and Rangers.

Hooton made his major league debut on June 17, 1971. His record was a modest 34-42 with the Cubs from 1971-75.

"The memory that sticks out for me was just my first day at Wrigley Field," said Hooton, who began the 2004 season as the pitching coach for the Houston Astros and has served as a minor league coach since his tenure with the Astros. "Coming off the University of Texas campus and into that Cubs clubhouse...I was just a 21-year-old kid. I was watching Ernie Banks and Billy Williams and Ron Santo and Don Kessinger and Glenn Beckert and Randy Hundley and Fergie Jenkins. These were guys that I had been watching on TV the previous eight or nine years. Then all of a sudden, here I am wearing the same uniform and I am one of their teammates. I will always remember just the way they accepted me and how nice and professional they all were."

Brace Photo

44 · BURT HOOTON · P
Years with Cubs: 1971-75

Won 14 games in 1973 • Posted 2.80 ERA with 11 wins in 1972 • Totaled 34 wins and made 129 appearances with Cubs

Hooton no-hit the Phillies on April 16, 1972, a 4-0 victory that featured no strikeouts and seven walks.

"Certainly, pitching the no-hitter was big," said Hooton, a six-foot, one-inch, 210-pound right-hander. "And the loyalty of the Cub fans is one of the things you always remember."

Renowned for keeping hitters off balance with a unique knuckle-curveball, "Happy" Hooton also was capable of raring back and firing a high hard one past a hitter.

"I started throwing the knuckle-curve when I was about 14 years old," said Hooton. "I had watched Hoyt Wilhelm pitch a game on *The Game of the Week* on TV. I decided I was at least going to experiment with it. I really didn't know how to throw one. I just kind of used common sense, thinking that if you are going to throw a knuckleball, you must put your knuckles down on the ball. Then I heard someone say that you push it out. I knew the ball was supposed to come out with no spin, but when I pushed it out with my knuckles on it, it came out with a forward spin on it. I never could throw a knuckleball, per se. With a knuckleball you dig your fingertips into the hide of the ball and push it out that way.

"I folded my fingertips underneath, but when I pushed, that's what put the rotation on it. The harder I threw it, it started breaking. I started using it in ballgames. I just developed it at an early age and stayed with it."

Hooton said he had no pregame plan regarding his knuckle-curveball usage.

"I threw the knuckle-curve whenever I needed it. I liked using the fastball. But I used the other pitch to keep them off the fastball," said Hooton. "So, some games I needed it more than I did in others."

Hooton didn't teach the knuckle-curve to his Houston Astros pitchers, and he rarely sees any current pitchers throughout the league attempting to throw it.

"I don't know of any pitchers who use the knuckle-curve today," he said in 2004. "I think Mike Mussina [of the Yankees] uses something similar, but I am not real certain about how he throws it. I don't think he throws it exactly the way I did. I can't be certain of that. Some people's definition of a knuckle-curve and what I threw are different things."

On May 2, 1975, Hooton was traded by the Cubs to the Los Angeles Dodgers for Geoff Zahn and Eddie Solomon.

"When I was with the Cubs, one of the reasons I probably had a little difficulty at a young age was because I had three different managers and four pitching coaches," said Hooton. "Consistency wasn't one of the things that was prevalent with the Cubs then. The best pitching coach that I ever had was a man by the name of Red Adams when I first went to Los Angeles. He had a knack for keeping things simple and keeping you within yourself. Basically, that's when guys perform the best. I was trying to do things with the Cubs that I wasn't familiar with. Consequently, I wasn't very good at it."

As a member of the Dodgers, Hooton went 18-7 in 1975 after beginning that season 0-2 with the Cubs. In 1978, he was 19-10 with a 3.51 earned run average. In 1981 he was the Most Valuable Player in the National League Championship Series, the same year that he was named to the NL All-Star team.

Hooton threw over 200 innings in nine different seasons, including over 239 with the Cubs in 1973. Asked his opinion as to why most young pitchers today don't approach those numbers, Hooton replied:

"Pitch counts, agents, lots of money, specialization in the bullpen. It's just the way kids are brought up.

"There are probably a few more hard throwers now. But we had a few hard throwers in our day," he said. "There have been hard throwers in all eras. My theory is that if you throw the ball right, you should be able to throw quite a few pitches without getting hurt."

On December 20, 1984, Hooton was signed as a free agent with the Texas Rangers for $690,000. He was released by the Rangers on March 27, 1986.

As the pitching coach for the Astros, Hooton was entrusted with working with 42-year-old future Hall of Famer Roger Clemens in 2004.

Hooton was fired right after the All-Star break. "He certainly doesn't act his age," said Houston manager Jimy Williams, who was also fired. "Those of us in Houston who have had a chance to see him, every one of these games, we need to appreciate what we are seeing here. It's something special. And we should enjoy it while we can. This kind of stuff doesn't come along all the time."

"Anything a Hall of Famer does amazes me," said Hooton. "They are fun to watch. I watched a few when I was pitching, and I have watched a few since. I was just proud to have him on our staff and see how he goes about his business. His preparation, physically and mentally...he just keeps himself prepared. That's a gift."

Clemens pitched for the Boston Red Sox (1984-1996), Toronto Blue Jays (1997-1998) and New York Yankees (1999-2003) before retiring, then later was persuaded to sign with his hometown Astros in January 2004.

He twice struck out 20 batters in a nine-inning game. On April 29, 1986, Clemens fanned 20 Mariners in a 3-1 Red Sox victory at Fenway Park. During one stretch in that outing, he struck out eight straight batters, tying an AL record held jointly by Nolan Ryan and Ron Davis. On September 18, 1996, he fanned 20 Tigers at Fenway Park. In 2001, at the age of 39, Clemens won 20 of his first 21 decisions en route to his sixth Cy Young award.

"He certainly has been a welcome addition to our team. He retired, but it wasn't like they say, he was 'over the hill,'" said Williams in 2004. "It wasn't like he had a bad year last year. He had a good year [13-6]. He retired; then he unretired. He has helped our ball club, not only with his ability on the mound there, but with his leadership, too."

Hooton figured Clemens made his job easier by providing a winning example for the younger Houston pitchers.

The success of the Astros' pitching staff was a positive reflection on the experience and expertise of Hooton.

RANDY HUNDLEY

He was known as "The Rebel," a good ol' boy from Martinsville, Virginia, who battled his opponents relentlessly and competed to the utmost of his ability as a scrappy catcher.

"I don't know who gave me that nickname 'The Rebel,'" said Randy Hundley, who played 10 of his 14 years in the big leagues with the Cubs. "It might have been the [Wrigley Field] Bleacher Bums. I guess with my Southern accent and being from the South, that was a part of it. And I don't know if my attitude was part of what they were thinking, also."

Hundley signed his first big-league contract in 1960.

"I originally signed with the Giants," said Hundley. "A scout from the Cubs was there when I was playing in high school, watching me play an awful lot. But the Cubs said they gave [bonus baby] Danny Murphy so much money that they couldn't afford any more for me. So the Cubs kind of dropped out of the bidding real early. Then I signed with San Francisco.

"I was sitting in sociology class at around two o'clock in the afternoon in about the middle of February. It was a very overcast day and I am sitting sideways in my chair, just dreaming of going to Florida for spring training. I am reading about these guys driving through my home town. I am thinking, 'Man, I should be going to spring training.'

Brace Photo

9/5/4 · RANDY HUNDLEY · C
Years with Cubs: 1966-73, 1976-77

All-Star in 1969 • NL Gold Glove in 1967 • Had career-high 19 HR in 1966 and 65 RBI in 1968 • Totaled 80 HR and 364 RBI with Cubs

"Then a knock comes on the door and the classroom is just out of control. This huge man approaches me and reaches out to shake my hand. He says, 'Randy, my name is Tim Murchison and I am a scout for the San Francisco Giants.'

"Well, you can just imagine what my heart did. And I had just started my junior year in high school. He had just seen me play between my sophomore and junior year during the summer in American Legion ball. The scout had been looking at the older kids, and I happened to have a good series.

"So I was able to sign for $110,000 with the Giants," said Hundley. "I played in the minor leagues and, of course, they didn't like my one-handed catching style.

"Bob Kennedy [of the Cubs organization] had scouted me and had seen me play at Triple A [for the Giants]. He recommended me to become Leo Durocher's catcher. That's how I got to the Cubs. Bill Hands and I came over."

Hundley played for the Cubs from 1966-73 and 1976-77 and was a Wrigley Field favorite. He occasionally does color commentary of Cubs games on WGN Radio.

"I am still doing the Fantasy Camps," said Hundley in 2004, after undergoing back surgery that spring. "This is going into our 22nd year of doing it. And I am trying to play as much golf as I possibly can. I am doing a lot of traveling since I lost my wife. I have been going quite a bit, just to stay out of the house. She passed away on Labor Day of 2000. So it has been pretty tough for me. I am still trying to catch up from that. I never had to handle the books before or the bills. It can really get away from you."

Hundley remains close with his former Cubs teammates.

"I think the Fantasy Camp has allowed us to stay close quite a bit," he said in 2004. "Also, we were good friends when we were playing. We played hard together. And it just remained that way. That was a different generation of players who remain friends today. Whereas the players of today, I am sure they will have some great friends, but they might not have as many."

One of Hundley's toughest adjustments when he joined the Cubs was playing for demanding manager Leo "The Lip" Durocher.

"It was a little intimidating for both Bill Hands and me because of Leo. Just his reputation," said Hundley. "After my first year, I thought, if I have to play like that...they can take this job and shove it. Because Leo was on my fanny every day. Then my second year with the Cubs, Leo came to me in spring training and said: 'Look, you have played for me for a year and you know how I want to play the game. You are the manager on the field. When you see something, you just go ahead and do it. You want to move somebody, you move them. If you have problems, you come to me.'

"He just turned me loose."

Hundley supplanted Dick Bertell as the Cubs' catcher when he was acquired from the Giants on December 2, 1965. The Cubs sent Lindy McDaniel and Don Landrum to San Francisco.

"I remember in 1966. I caught 149 games and I ended up hitting 19 home runs. I thought I was going to hit about 30. But the heat got to me and I couldn't even reach the warning track. Other than having to put up with the stuff from Leo, I enjoyed my rookie year," said Hundley.

Hundley is most frequently asked about the 1969 Cubs team that blew a huge lead in August and finished second to the New York Mets.

On August 13, 1969, the Cubs held a nine and a half-game lead over the Mets. Two weeks later, the lead was down to two games. The Cubs would then lose eight in a row in September while the Mets won 10 in a row. The Cubs finished eight games out of first place.

"I don't know, to be honest with you, what could have made the difference in 1969," said Hundley. "I know that we wore [reliever] Phil Regan out. And our bullpen after that didn't have much work, so I think they were not real comfortable with the role after we somewhat lost Regan. Then it was bullpen by committee, and that just didn't work out for us. Of course, we didn't hit that well down the stretch, either.

"Sometimes it's just destiny. You always win with pitching and defense. When you look at the Mets, they had pitching and defense. The other thing that I think helped them a lot was acquiring Don Clendenon. He carried them a number of games down the stretch. Since then I have gotten to known Don Clendenon and I now know he had a big influence in the clubhouse. Because he is really just a strong person and a good human being."

One of the most enduring images that depicted the Cubs' frustration in 1969 was Hundley hopping up and down at home plate following a disputed call at home plate against the Mets in New York's Shea Stadium.

"Bill Hands was our pitcher in that game," said Hundley. "The first pitch of the ballgame, he knocks Tommy Agee right on his fanny. Bill and I had not even talked about doing that. But I thought: 'Man, this is great. This is what we're here for.'

"But Tommy Agee casually got up, brushed himself off. He didn't seem to be too upset. I think the count went to two balls and one strike. And Bill Hands threw him one of the best sliders, and in the best spot, that you could throw it. And Agee takes the pitch over the center field wall. So I'm thinking, 'Oh, no. We just woke his fanny up.'

"Then we tied the game somehow or another, and I think that was the game where [Mets pitcher] Jerry Koosman hit Ron Santo, after we had knocked down Agee. The Mets let us know that they weren't going to sit back and take anything.

"The big controversial play involved us pitching to Wayne Garrett and trying to just keep the ball in the infield with two outs. Before I could get the thought out of my head, he has hit a pretty good pitch to right field. Jim Hickman makes a great throw to the plate and it is up the line a little bit. I catch it and I tag Tommy all the way from his thighs all the way up to his chin almost. The problem is that the umpire was on the other side of it and he had Agee between him and me.

"The way that I had to swipe at him, the umpire evidently thought that I had missed him. But I had tagged him so hard that I almost dropped the ball. The ball went up in the webbing of my mitt and I was able to hold on. Whenever you see the replay, you realize that players are not actors. If I had missed the tag, what's the first thing I am going to do? I am going to go back and try to tag him.

"So I tagged Agee [the first time], and I turned around to make sure the runner didn't go to second base. [Garrett] saw me tag Agee and he is looking disgusted down at first. Then all of a sudden I hear this tremendous roar go up and I said: 'Oh, no, I can't believe this.'

"I turned and Satch Davidson has got the safe sign going down. I just went berserk. I knew I had to jump up and down in order to stay away and not make contact with him, or else I would be suspended.

"The Mets won that ballgame [3-2] and it was a big swing game for us. I knew that right then and there that this was going to be a big play. I knew it was going to be a big play for the entire season. The Mets had to know that they did get a big break there."

Many baseball observers feel the Cubs also could have contended in 1970 and '71 if they had made it to the World Series in 1969.

"I think we had the nucleus of a ball club to win the title numerous times," said Hundley. "I believe 80 percent of that game of baseball is in your head. If you go out there and play and feel like you are not going to get the breaks or whatever, then you are just making it tougher on yourself. And I think at times we made it a little bit tougher on ourselves than we needed to. You know, just go play the game and give it every stinkin' thing you've got and don't worry about the breaks that go against you. Somewhere along the way they will come back to your side. But with Leo it made it tough because he wanted to fight and fuss about every bloomin' thing."

On December 6, 1973, Hundley was traded by the Cubs to the Minnesota Twins for catcher George Mitterwald.

Hundley was released by the Twins on October 25, 1974. On April 3, 1975, he was signed as a free agent with the San Diego Padres. His contract was purchased by the Cubs again on April 13, 1976. The Cubs released him a final time on October 12, 1977.

A .236 career hitter, Hundley had 82 career homers. His son, Todd Hundley, followed him into the big leagues as a catcher.

"When Todd got into playing ball, he said: 'Dad, what would you do differently if you had it to do again?'

"I said, 'Son, I would not let every pitch be a matter of life and death with me in a ballgame. It's just not that important and it makes your life miserable.'

"That's what Leo wanted, and that's how I had to play the game. I just got a bad reputation, because every day Leo would want me to rag on those umpires. 'Get on 'em so you can make them mad enough so I can come out and protect you,' Leo would say. Then Leo would tell me, 'If you don't do it, then I will get somebody else back there who will.'

"It made it tough for me. It made it tough hitting because I had times I didn't get pitches we should have gotten."

Todd Hundley, a two-time All-Star, put up impressive power numbers as a catcher with the Mets and Dodgers early in his career. He hit 41 home runs as a member of the Mets in 1996, setting a major league record for home runs by a catcher.

Todd Hundley hit 24 homers and drove in 70 runs in only 90 games the year before joining the Cubs. He struggled in the field, throwing out 20 percent of base stealers last season. The Dodgers didn't offer him salary arbitration.

Todd had agreed to a $23.5 million, four-year deal to sign with the Cubs. But he struggled mightily as a member of the Cubs and was booed by the Wrigley Field faithful before being traded back to the Dodgers for Eric Karros and Mark Grudzielanek before the 2003 season.

"I looked at the situation here in Chicago at the time when Todd was free agent," said Randy Hundley. "I looked at left field, I looked at right field, I looked at center field...and knowing the power that Todd had to all of those fields...I just thought it was a perfect fit for him. And he wanted to be in Chicago. My wife had passed away in September [2000]. And now it is December. I could hear my wife say, 'No, no, no, no...don't do it, don't do it.' And I felt those instincts that she always had for Todd playing here. And I kind of went against those instincts. Sometimes I think that was one of the reasons that Todd struggled, because I didn't listen to my wife's instincts.

"But I also looked at the situation. I thought Don Baylor was going to be a great manager. I thought Don Baylor would love Todd Hundley and the player he was. And I thought that [incumbent Cubs catcher] Joe Girardi was becoming a journeyman catcher. A good guy to have on the ball club. A backup-type guy, but certainly not a starter or anything near an everyday player.

"So when I analyzed all of that, I just thought it was a perfect place for Todd. And he wanted to be in Chicago and close to his family after the loss of my wife. But I think Todd actually suffered from depression. I don't think he knew what it was. I don't think he knew what to do about it, how to handle it. What medications to use for it.

"Then when you top it off and you come here and [Todd] doesn't start the season as the opening day catcher, it sends a bad message. It made me sick as a dog," said Hundley. "I was absolutely livid, to be honest with you."

Like any proud father, Randy Hundley wanted desperately for his son to succeed in Chicago. Todd batted .187 and .211 his first two seasons with the Cubs.

"I think at times Todd hurt himself in spring training," Randy said. "I had always told Todd throughout his career: 'Be the first one there and be the last at the park.' I think he had done that for a lot of years. But when he was in spring training with the Cubs…"

Todd Hundley had established a reputation with the Mets of partying and drinking heavily. He even publicly admitted to those excesses. When Todd began to struggle on the field with the Cubs, rumors surfaced again that he was spending too much time enjoying the nightlife.

"He didn't do anything close to the stuff that he was accused of doing," said Randy Hundley. "I just think he was suffering from depression. Sometimes when you get that, you cannot put a foot on the floor. If he wasn't late getting to the park, it was awfully close. That may have set [former Cubs manager] Don Baylor off, or whatever. As a dad, I had to get him up to go to practice in the morning to try to get him there on time. But I can tell you one thing, it wasn't from him being out and hounding and drinking and partying whatsoever. He was very serious about it. He wanted to succeed.

"I was just learning to deal with [depression] myself. I didn't know what the heck was hitting me. I mean, think about it. All I wanted to do was to get to Arizona and be with Todd. He would go work out. I would go hit golf balls. But I only went to hit golf balls two times the whole spring training. I just couldn't get out of bed. And after Todd's game was over, I would come back to the hotel and I just wanted to stay in my room. They tell me now that that is a matter of depression."

"You have to mourn," said Hundley in 2004. "I was able to mourn my wife's death because I took care of her every day. She passed away here in my house. So I grieved with her every stinkin' day. Todd had said good-bye to her about three times before she passed away. It had to be tough on him. He was still in-season with the Dodgers at the time. I don't think he really had a chance to grieve her death. Being there a couple times helped him a little. He knew she was going to die. You just don't know what it is going to do to you.

"I buried my wife on a Thursday. And on Monday night I am in a grief support session. Well, guess where Todd was? Behind the plate in Los Angeles. I just didn't think he had the opportunity to grieve the loss of his mother.

"By no means, I don't want to sound like I am making any excuses. There were times that things were said, that things were printed that I know for a fact were nowhere close to being correct. I had to bite my tongue. There were some times when I wanted to take some people's heads off. It made it real difficult on Todd. And even to this day, I don't know why Don Baylor didn't like Todd. I thought it would be a perfect situation for both of them.

"I have always wanted Todd to play for Dusty Baker," Hundley said in 2004. "There was a time when he was a free agent, I wanted him to play in San Francisco for Dusty Baker."

DARRIN JACKSON

A second-round draft pick of the Cubs in 1981, outfielder Darrin Jackson enjoyed modest success in the major leagues. He is better known these days as a broadcaster for Chicago White Sox games.

Jackson made his major league debut June 17, 1985, at New York. He collected his first career hit off Ed Lynch of the Mets.

"I remember facing Ron Darling of the Mets in my first big-league game. My second game was against Dwight Gooden and my third game was against Ed Lynch," recalled Jackson. "I ended up getting my first big-league hit off the former general manager of the Cubs—a line drive over the second baseman. Everytime Ed Lynch sees me, he says: 'Yeah, yeah, I know.' That was my claim to fame in 1985."

Jackson spent five games with the Cubs that first year before returning to Pittsfield. He also spent the 1986 season at Pittsfield, and was named to the Eastern League's All-Star team.

Recalled from Triple A Iowa September 4, 1987, Jackson underwent surgery September 21 to remove a small tumor from his groin area and missed the rest of the season. He had batted .800 (four for five) with one double for the Cubs.

Jackson played center field for both the Cubs and White Sox, with a career batting average of .257 over 960 career games that also included

Brace Photo

30 · DARRIN JACKSON · OF
Years with Cubs: 1985-89

Hit .266 with 6 HR and 20 RBI in 100 games in 1988 • Totaled 7 HR and 28 RBI in 157 games with Cubs

stints with the San Diego Padres, Toronto Blue Jays, Minnesota Twins, Milwaukee Brewers and Mets. Jackson recalls fondly the atmosphere in Chicago when he played in the Cubs-Sox regular-season games in 1999.

"The biggest thing to me was that the energy and the excitement was there," said Jackson. "The fans were so pumped up and so divided. That translated into how you felt and played on the field. You really get motivated to do a good job. The first time I ever played in that type of game [as an exhibition], it was called the old Windy City Classic. It was high energy for three days and actually draining. You looked forward to it, and then you were glad it was done. I was in a White Sox uniform in '99, and [the Cubs] played a little better than we did. There were some close games. But in '99 they were a better team and it showed."

Jackson completed his 12th year as a Sox broadcaster and currently works with veteran play-by-play man Ed Farmer.

He previously worked alongside Ken "Hawk" Harrelson for eight years. "Hawk has always been there for me," said Jackson in 2004. "He is the same person I knew when I was a player [with the White Sox] in 1994. The difference is that he has been a teacher and somebody who has helped me with the little things to improve in this industry. Hawk and I have always had a lot of fun away from the park, going out to eat together and such. That is one of the things people don't realize. Sometimes it seems like we butt heads on the air, but that's just because we might have a difference of opinion on something. It has nothing to do with how we get along. In broadcasting, it's just like when I played. Each day I want to go out and have the best game I can. It's hard to do that. The game determines so much in terms of the direction of a broadcast.

"We're here every day with the guys and we see what goes on with the team. We want them to succeed and have nothing but winning ways."

Darrin Jay Jackson was born August 22, 1963, in Los Angeles. He graduated from Culver City High School in 1981, after lettering in football, basketball and baseball. As a senior, he was one of three California players named to the High School All-America first team.

The six-foot, 185-pound Jackson appeared in 100 games for the Cubs in 1988, but had only 188 at-bats. He became the third player in Cubs history (joining Dale Long and Carmen Fanzone) to homer in consecutive pinch-hit at-bats. He homered against St. Louis's Ken Dayley on August 14, 1988, and Cincinnati's Tom Browning August 16. He had the first two-homer game of his career September 17 against St. Louis.

The 1989 season also saw Jackson splitting time between the Cubs and Triple A Iowa. He was finally traded to San Diego on August 31, 1989, and made 23 starts for the Padres. Since he was traded to San Diego, Jackson missed out when it came to playing in the postseason with the Cubs.

The 1989 Cubs finished 17-11 in September and won their second NL Eastern Division championship.

Led by manager Don Zimmer, the '89 Cubs enjoyed All-Star seasons from Ryne Sandberg, Andre Dawson, Rick Sutcliffe along with relief pitcher Mitch Williams and a Rookie of the Year performance by center fielder Jerome Walton. The San Francisco Giants defeated the Cubs in the NLCS four games to one.

The 1990 season also saw Jackson splitting his time between the minors (Triple A Las Vegas) and the big-league club. But he did manage to hit the Padres' first pinch-hit homer of the season on April 27, 1990, against Pittsburgh. Then he had his first career four-hit game October 3 at Los Angeles.

Jackson enjoyed a breakthrough season in 1991, hitting a career-high 21 home runs in 122 games after entering the season with a career total of 13. He ranked fourth in the National League with one homer for every 17 at-bats. During one 19-game stretch between June 9 and July 12 of 1991, seven of his 11 hits were homers. Jackson blasted his first career grand slam August 25 off the Cubs' Bob Scanlan. Just to spice things up, Jackson made his only career pitching appearance with two innings at Houston on May 26, 1991.

More opportunities to play led to more success on the field for Jackson the following season in San Diego.

He set career highs in games (155), RBIs (70), hits (146) and stolen bases (14) in 1992. Jackson tied his career high with four hits in two games, July 7 against St. Louis, and July 19 at Montreal. He had his fourth career two-homer game April 28 against Philadelphia, the second homer leading off the bottom of the ninth and giving the Padres a 7-6 victory. And he had three game-winning homers on the season. Defensively, Jackson tied for second among National League outfielders with a .996 fielding percentage, a San Diego club record. He also led the majors with 18 outfield assists.

But 1993 proved to be a difficult year for Jackson. He was with San Diego for spring training, with Toronto until June 11 and with the New York Mets for the rest of the season.

His solo homer in the eighth inning off the White Sox' Alex Fernandez April 25, 1993, was the difference in a 1-0 Toronto victory.

But he struggled at the plate most of the season, hitting .216 for the Blue Jays and .195 for the Mets. He did not commit an error in 23 outfield starts with the Mets, handling 55 chances. But Jackson spent July 19-September 1 on the disabled list with hyperthyroidism.

Jackson batted a career-high .312 in 87 games with the White Sox in 1994. That promising season for Jackson and the White Sox ended unfulfilled on August 12, because major league players walked out on strike. The work stoppage also wiped out the playoffs and the World Series. When play on the field concluded, the White Sox were in first place with a 67-42 record. That ended Jackson's best chance to play in a World Series during his 12-year major league career.

Jackson continued his professional baseball stint playing in Japan. He signed with the Seibu Lions of Japanese Pacific League and ranked seventh in the league with a .289 average. He hit 20 home runs and drove in 68 runs.

In 1996 he hit .266 with 19 home runs and 64 RBIs in 126 games for the Seibu Lions.

Jackson returned to the major leagues in 1997 to play for the Minnesota Twins and Milwaukee Brewers during the next two seasons. He enjoyed his second stint with the White Sox in 1999, hitting .275 in 73 games.

Jackson, who married Robin during the 2003 offseason, has four children: Alexandre, Arianna, Adian, and Tatum.

Jackson has been involved in several off-field initiatives, including "Project I Believe," a program that focuses on improving the confidence and self-esteem of minority youngsters.

FERGUSON JENKINS

One of the greatest pitchers never to have pitched in the postseason, Ferguson Jenkins started six home openers for the Cubs during his Hall of Fame career and is one of the only major league pitchers to record 3,000 strikeouts while issuing fewer than 1,000 walks.

Jenkins, who later served as a pitching coach with the Cubs said in 2004 that he had no immediate aspirations to return to the big leagues in any capacity.

"No, not really. My wife and I are pretty happy here in Guthrie, Oklahoma," he said. "I have 160 acres, raising horses and cattle. I coached for eight years—Cincinnati, Texas and Chicago. You know, you try to give something back. I tried to hand the information that was given to me during my career back to these young men."

Jenkins wound up his 19-year playing career with an impressive 3.34 earned run average, even though he pitched 12 of those seasons in hitters' ballparks Wrigley Field and Fenway Park. Jenkins does not quite understand why so many other Cubs pitchers seem to psyche themselves out in Wrigley Field.

"The first thing is that you can't be afraid of the ballpark," Jenkins said. "I first came up [with the Phillies] and Connie Mack was a very small ballpark. Then Wrigley is small. There were so many smaller parks

Brace Photo

31 · FERGUSON JENKINS · P
Years with Cubs: 1966-73, 1982-83

**Three-time All-Star • 1971 NL Cy Young Award • Led NL with 24 wins
and 325.0 innings in 1971 • Led NL with 273 strikeouts in 1969 • Led
NL in complete games three times • Six-time 20-game winner with Cubs
• Totaled 167 wins and 149 CG in 334 games with the Cubs • Elected to
Baseball Hall of Fame in 1991**

in the '60s. If Wrigley is your home ballpark, you have to feel comfortable with that situation because you can't change it. You have to pitch accordingly. You take a certain game plan and stick to it from the first inning through the ninth."

Having served as the Cubs' pitching coach in 1995-96, Jenkins knows how important is it to have complete coordination between the manager, pitching coach and pitchers when dealing with a staff.

"I think you have to have the working abilities of all three. The majority rules and a lot of times you get overturned. I just think that if the young man has the game in control and he is working to his best ability, there is no reason to take him out. But you see it done day after day. I have seen it as a pitching coach," he said.

Jenkins won 284 games for the Cubs, Phillies, Rangers and Red Sox and reached the 20-win mark seven seasons, capturing the National League Cy Young Award in 1971. It disappoints him now to see that starting pitchers who last just six innings and give up three runs are considered quality performers.

"If you address the fact that these young men can only go six innings, that is what you will see," he said in 2004. "But I think the Cubs have some strong individuals now. Kerry Wood is a big man, and so is Mark Prior. Carlos Zambrano is huge and he's all man with an excellent arm. I just think you have to give some of these young men a chance to pitch. If you only want to use the closer in the ninth inning, fine. But if you need the holder and then the setup man and then the closer...I don't think you need three more pitchers to save or win a ballgame."

Jenkins entered each game he pitched with a solid mental approach, as well as a strong physical plan.

"I pitched so many years in Wrigley Field with Randy Hundley and with J.C. Martin and a few other guys catching me. My strength was down. I just proved to the umpire that I could stay there. I think that is one of the things these pitchers need to do for their best interests. You have to show the umpire that you can do it on a daily basis. It's control, changing speeds and location."

Jenkins was able to pitch 300 innings five different seasons. He is befuddled by the fact so many pitchers seem to come down with injuries these days.

"I don't think they throw enough. They don't throw enough between starts," said Jenkins in 2004. "By far, they don't throw enough in spring training. I think the minor leagues are where you potentially groom a pitcher. A lot of young players get four games in Double A, skip to Triple A and then they are in the big leagues. When I played in the '60s, you had a whole season at Double A and a whole season at Triple A before you got promoted. So you could handle the pressure of playing at the big-league level. But they are operating now under the thinking that their top prospects are wasting their ability in the minor leagues."

In 2003, Jenkins served as the commissioner of a new league in his native Canada.

"We started a league in eight cities, and it is called the Canadian Baseball League. It is an independent league that is the equivalent to a little better than Double A ball, I think. You are going to see some ex-major leaguers, more minor leaguers and some amateurs right out of college looking to impress some [major league] scouts to get signed or re-signed with other organizations. That type of thing. I think Canada, in some cases, has been overlooked," said Jenkins.

For several years, Jenkins has conducted his annual Chicago area baseball and softball camp. Over the years, several of the camp counselors included Glenn Beckert, Bill Melton, Pete LaCock and Bob Dernier, as well as Jenkins.

Jenkins won 20 games six straight years and seven times overall. Yet he never played on a first-place team and did not gain the spotlight of playing in the postseason. A drug bust in 1980 tainted Jenkins's image, but 11 years later he was voted into the Hall of Fame.

He was named an All-Star three times: 1967, 1971 and '72. During an eight-year stretch, from 1967-1974, Jenkins finished in the top three in NL Cy Young voting five times. In 1967 he was runner-up to Mike McCormick, and in 1974 he was second to Catfish Hunter.

Jenkins was the consummate starting pitcher, even though the Phillies tried to make him a relief pitcher in his first two seasons in the major leagues. He made his major league debut September 10, 1965.

No doubt, Jenkins would have won 300 games if he had pitched for better teams. He lost 13 games by the score of 1-0, despite going the distance for the loss. Jenkins also endured 45 shutout losses, the sixth highest total in history. His teams (Phillies, Cubs, Rangers, and Red Sox) recorded an almost exact .500 record in games Jenkins didn't get a decision.

Talk about poor timing...in 1969, his Cubs blew a lead and lost the division title to the Mets. In 1976 Jenkins joined Boston the season after they played in the World Series. With the Rangers he was never able to get to the postseason. In 1983 he retired with the Cubs, and the next season they finished first in their division.

Jenkins was born in Canada and grew up playing hockey. He didn't become a pitcher until a teammate hurt his arm and Jenkins was forced into action. He was signed to his first pro contract on June, 1962, by the Phillies. In four seasons in the minors, Jenkins went 43-26.

After beginning the '66 season in the Phillies' bullpen, he was packaged in a deal with the Cubs. The Phillies traded Jenkins, Adolpho Phillips, and John Herrnstein to the Cubs for pitchers Larry Jackson and Bob Buhl. It would become one of the worst trades in baseball history.

In his first game with the Cubs, Jenkins clubbed a home run and won the contest in relief. He was inserted in the rotation later in the year, winning six games. In 1967 he won 20 games for the first time, and followed that up with 20, 21, 22, 24, and 20 wins the next five years, through 1972. In 1971 he earned the Cy Young award with a 24-13 record, 2.77 earned run average and 263 strikeouts.

Jenkins's remarkable string of 20-win seasons ended in 1973 (14-16), and the Cubs traded him to the Rangers for third baseman Bill Madlock. It was with Texas in '74 that Jenkins won a career-high 25 games and was voted the Comeback Player of the Year. In his first start with Texas, he blanked Oakland 2-0, on one hit.

After winning 17 games for the Texas in 1975, Jenkins was dealt to Boston. He managed just a 22-21 record in two seasons with the Red Sox. He was sent back to Texas, where he joined a staff that included Jon Matlack, Doyle Alexander and Gaylord Perry.

During his second tour of duty with Texas, Jenkins went 51-42 over four years.

The lone personal blemish of Jenkins's career came on August 25, 1980, in Toronto. Jenkins was arrested for possession of cocaine at Exhibition Stadium. The negative publicity and short trial caused a a bit of commotion in Canada, where Jenkins is a hero. A judge waived a guilty verdict against Jenkins. After Major League Baseball suspended him in September, 1980, that ruling also was overturned after an arbitrator dismissed the claim.

Jenkins became a free agent after the '81 season. The Cubs re-signed the 38-year-old right-hander. He won 14 games with an impressive 3.15 ERA in 1982. He finished up in 1983, winding up in the Cubs' bullpen.

His career was marked by his incredible durability and control. In 1991 he was inducted into the Hall of Fame along with Gaylord Perry and Rod Carew.

DON KESSINGER

One of the most consistent, yet at times overlooked, standouts with the Cubs during the 1960s and '70s, Don Kessinger patrolled the shortstop position with authority.

During his 16-year major league career, Kessinger led National League shortstops in putouts three years, assists four years, double plays four years and fielding percentage once. He played 54 errorless games in 1969, which was then a record for big-league shortstops. He started for the NL in five All-Star Games.

He was a career .252 hitter with only 14 home runs. But his sparkling defense made him the cornerstone of the Cubs' infield that included Ron Santo at third base, Glenn Beckert at second and Ernie Banks at first.

Kessinger's highest batting average came in 1966 and 1972 when he hit .274. And on July 17, 1970, he went six for six in a 10-inning game.

Born July 17, 1942, in Forrest City, Arkansas, Donald Eulon Kessinger signed with the Cubs out of the University of Mississippi for $25,000. He made his major league debut on September 7, 1964.

In 1969, Kessinger hit .273 to help the Cubs lead their division most of the season. On August 13, 1969, the Cubs staked themselves to a nine

Brace Photo

11 · DON KESSINGER · SS
Years with Cubs: 1964-1975

Six-time All-Star • NL Gold Glove in 1969 and 1970 • Was second in NL with 38 doubles, fourth with 109 runs scored and seventh with 181 hits in 1969 • Scored 100 runs twice with the Cubs • Totaled 769 runs scored and 431 RBI with Cubs

and a half-game lead over the New York Mets. The lead was reduced to two games two weeks later.

The Cubs would lose eight in a row in September while the Mets won 10 in a row. The Cubs finished eight games out of first place, and they missed the playoffs again following one of the worst collapses in baseball history.

Entering the 2013 season, the Cubs hadn't been to the World Series since 1945. They failed to make the playoffs between 1945 and 1984, a period of 39 years. The Cubs did manage to earn playoff berths in 1984, 1989, 1998, and 2003, when they won a playoff round (against Atlanta) for the first time in over 50 years. Subsequently, they made consecutive playoff appearances in 2007 and 2008.

But the disappointment of the 1969 season still resonates with Cubs fans.

In the opener at Wrigley Field in '69, the Cubs fell behind the Phillies 6-5 and had one on in the 11th inning when Willie Smith stepped to the plate. Smith hit a pinch home run into the right field bleachers to give the Cubs the victory. The Cubs then would not fall out of first place for 155 days.

On May 13, 1969, Ernie Banks had seven RBIs, including his 1,500th on a three-run homer during a 19-0 blowout of San Diego. It matched the biggest shutout margin in major league history. Cubs pitcher Dick Selma took the victory with his three-hit performance. The Cubs had obtained Selma from the Padres earlier in the season. It was the third straight shutout thrown by Cubs pitchers. Ferguson Jenkins and Ken Holtzman preceded Selma's gem.

A week later, the Cubs blanked the Dodgers 7-0 in Los Angeles behind Holtzman. It was the 12th loss in a row by the Dodgers' Don Sutton in contests against the Cubs.

On June 15, 1969, Kessinger set a National League record with his 54th straight errorless game to start the season. But the Cubs dropped a 7-6 decision in the first game of a doubleheader in Cincinnati.

On July 14, the Cubs edged the Mets 1-0 behind Bill Hands's win against Tom Seaver. Billy Williams singled home the game winner to give the Cubs a five and a half-game lead over the Mets. At the end of the game, Cubs third baseman Ron Santo infuriated the Mets by jumping up and clicking his heels in glee as the Chicago crowd roared its approval.

On "Billy Williams Day" (June 29) at Wrigley Field, Williams passed Stan Musial's NL record for consecutive games played (896). The Cubs swept the Cardinals 3-1 and 12-1 in front of 41,060 fans.

In a memorable 4-3 loss to the Mets on July 8, Ron Santo criticized center fielder Don Young for two misplays in the outfield. Santo apologized the next day for ripping into Young, who had left the park early and did not take the team bus. But Santo was booed by the home crowd in his first game back at Wrigley Field.

Holtzman pitched the fifth no-hitter in the majors of 1969 on August 19 against the Braves. Holtzman no-hit Atlanta despite failing to strike out a single batter in the 3-0 victory. Williams hauled in a deep drive hit by Hank Aaron against the left field vines in the seventh inning to help preserve the no-hitter.

By August 27, the Cubs' lead over the Mets had slipped to two games. A 6-3 loss to the Reds was the Cubs' seventh in their last eight games.

The Cubs dropped to second place on September 10 after losing to the Phillies 6-2. The Cubs were out of first place after spending 155 days atop the National League East. Meanwhile, the Mets swept the Montreal Expos, 3-2 and 7-1, to take a one-game lead in the division.

The Cubs would continue to swoon and wound up with a 9-17 record in the month of September. Their final record was 92-70. Jenkins would wind up with a 21-15 record and a 3.41 ERA. Hands was 20-14, 2.29. Holtzman checked in with a 17-13 record and a 3.58 ERA. Reliever Phil Regan had a 12-6 record and 17 saves.

Former Cubs general manager E.R. "Salty" Saltwell traded Kessinger to the St. Louis Cardinals on October 28, 1975, for reliever Mike Garman and a minor leaguer. In 1977 he was dealt to the Chicago White Sox.

But Kessinger's most significant career change occurred three years later. On October 19, 1978, the White Sox fired manager Larry Doby and named Kessinger as player-manager for the 1979 season.

Kessinger admits it was a difficult transition becoming the White Sox player/manager in 1979 as a 37-year-old shortstop. He draws parallels between his experience as a young manager with current White Sox manager Ozzie Guillen, who took over in 2004 at the age of 39.

"It is difficult when you have played with people and then you turn around and are going to be their boss, so to speak," said Kessinger. "But Ozzie commands a lot of respect, and I don't think he will have any problems. What you have to be careful of is that you are not overly concerned with personalities. You just have to do what's best for the ball club. After you have been very close to individuals, then it is a little bit more difficult. But I think his age is a plus, to be honest with you. I think he will relate really well with all of the players."

Kessinger's 1979 White Sox team struggled (46-60), and eventually Tony La Russa took over as manager. Kessinger felt conflicted during his tour of duty when it came to penciling himself into the White Sox line-up.

"The most difficult thing for me—and part of it was my personality... I never wanted people to think that I was playing because I was the manager," Kessinger said. "My coaches told me repeatedly: 'You really need to be playing more.' I just kind of fought that a little bit. It was more difficult to me being a player/manager than the actual managing part was. I don't think Ozzie will have any problems with that sort of thing. It is also important to have a very good bench coach. I think he needs to pick someone that he has great faith in. The '79 season was a great experience for me. Toward the end of [former Sox owner] Bill Veeck's deal, we really did not have the money to go into that free agent market and compete. We were, at times, trying to play six or seven designated hitters. To me, that was the most difficult part about it."

While he experienced many memorable moments with the Cubs—including the near-pennant in 1969—Kessinger will never forget the 1979 White Sox season, either.

"I don't know, I guess 'Disco Demolition Night' sticks out," he said of the record-burning promotion that got out of hand at old Comiskey Park.

"It was just such an unbelievable deal. I just wanted to make sure that night that we got all of the players out of the dugout and into the locker room between games of that doubleheader. I had the door locked so nobody could get in or out. I will never forget the umpires coming up to me and saying that they needed to find Bill Veeck. But Bill was out in the middle of the field [where thousands of disco records were on fire] with a microphone saying: 'Will you please return to your seats.' It was a tough night, I will say that. I think it was one of those promotions that was too successful. [Disc jockey] Steve Dahl commanded an awful lot of attention. I knew that night, prior to the game, that we had a problem. It was just a different night because at least half the fans were there for something other than a baseball game. I knew there was a potential problem. They made us forfeit the second game of the doubleheader. Those are the experiences I will never forget as a manager."

Since retiring from the MLB, Kessinger has worked in the insurance and real estate businesses.

DAVE KINGMAN

DAVE KINGMAN

One of the game's most enigmatic sluggers, Dave Kingman created a spotlight for himself with the Cubs that he tried to shun throughout his career.

The six-foot, six-inch Kingman was nicknamed "King Kong" in 1979 when he belted a major league-high 48 home runs, many of which were the most prodigious in Wrigley Field history.

Kingman played for the San Francisco Giants (1971-1974), New York Mets (1975-1977, 1981-1983), California Angels (1977), New York Yankees (1977), San Diego Padres (1977), Cubs (1978-1980) and Oakland A's (1984-1986), totaling 442 career homers.

Every at-bat was a dramatic adventure for Kingman, whose awesome swings made him particularly susceptible to striking out.

"Everybody's always talking about my strikeouts. If I played every day, I could strike out maybe 400 times. I have no idea how many home runs I could hit if I played every day. I've never played every day," Kingman said in 1975.

Kingman had an adversarial relationship with the media throughout his career. He dumped a bucket of ice water over the head of a Chicago sportswriter during spring training in Arizona. As a member of the A's,

Brace Photo

10 · DAVE KINGMAN · OF
Years with Cubs: 1978-80

Two-time All-Star • Led NL with 48 HR and .613 slugging percentage and was second with 115 RBI in 1979 • Hit 94 HR and totaled 251 RBI with Cubs.

he once was accused of sending a box with a dead rat in it to a female sportswriter.

While Kingman appeared aloof to media and some teammates, he had a friend and confidante in former Cubs trainer Tony Garofalo.

"I had a bunch of favorite guys, like Bruce Sutter, Rick Reuschel, Rick Sutcliffe, Jody Davis, Keith Moreland and Dave Kingman," said Garofalo. "We had a great relationship. Like Keith said, 'We were like brothers.' Part of the job was taking care of their physical problems. And a lot of the time you listen to their mental problems, too. You are surprised at how much people open up to you when you are one on one with them and you are rubbing on their shoulders or rubbing on their elbows. You learn a lot about them and their families and the different problems they have."

Kingman, 64, seems to have mellowed while living near Lake Tahoe, California.

"I have some great memories from playing with the Cubs and at Wrigley Field," Kingman said at a Cubs Fans Convention in Chicago several years ago.

"He was a bomber," said former Cubs interim manager Bruce Kimm, a teammate of Kingman's in 1979. "He had a wide stance, but he could hit the ball a long ways and he could run like heck."

In one of the most memorable games at Wrigley Field when the wind was blowing out, Kingman hit three home runs and drove in six on May 17, 1979, against Philadelphia. The Phillies prevailed 23-22. Hall of Fame third baseman Mike Schmidt hit two home runs that day for the Phillies, including the game-winning blast in the 10th inning.

In 1976 when he played for the New York Mets, Kingman blasted a home run that landed four houses down Kenmore Avenue, a street that runs into Wrigley's left-field bleachers. Cubs fans marked the spot with an "X" on the street.

Kingman was named to the All-Star team in 1976, 1979 and 1980. He was the American League Comeback Player of the Year in 1984. He hit three homers in a game five times, one shy of the major league record held by Johnny Mize.

On April 16, 1972, Kingman hit for the cycle while playing for the Giants.

The Giants sold Kingman to the Mets in March, 1975. Owner Horace Stoneham explained the deal: "He wasn't happy here, and we don't want him if he doesn't have a complete desire to be with us."

The Mets gave the Giants $100,000 for Kingman and made certain he knew his role on the club.

"What I saw of him at third I didn't like," said former Mets manager Yogi Berra. "But he gives us a pretty good guy on the bench and he's insurance in the outfield if Cleon Jones can't do the job."

Two years earlier, the Giants had tried unsuccessfully to trade Kingman straight up for Jon Matlack. But the Mets balked. The Mets said they were willing to deal pitcher Jerry Koosman, but the deal fell through.

The late Bobby Bonds thought Kingman's power potential was virtually limitless.

"I told Yogi that if he plays Dave in 150 games, he'll hit 30 homers for them, maybe 40. And after he's playing regularly for a couple of years, he'll be the next man to hit 60 homers," said Bonds in 1975.

But Kingman's best season overall was clearly 1979 with the Cubs, even though he struck out 131 times.

In his first full season for the Cubs, Kingman hit 48 homers and batted .288. He drove in 115 runs and scored 97. His .613 slugging percentage was almost 50 points higher than the next closest slugger-Schmidt.

The 1979 Cubs opened the season with four straight losses and finished the campaign with an 80-82 record. The Cubs were 16-8 in the month of June, 18-13 in July, and 17-14 in August. But a 9-22 mark in September ended any hope of contending. They had a 45-36 (.556 winning percentage) record at home and were 35-46 (.432 winning percentage) on the road.

Kingman hit three home runs in a game twice in 1979, once against the Phillies and the other time against the Mets.

He also hit five home runs over two consecutive games to tie a major league record.

In 1980, Kingman suffered a freak accident. He slipped on a bat after crossing home plate on May 30th and suffered a shoulder injury. He went on the injured list, and even his much-publicized column in the *Chicago Tribune* was discontinued. The Cubs plummeted to the NL East cellar without Kingman's bat and won only 64 games.

Still, Kingman was named to the National League All-Star team for the third time in his career. He struck out in his only at-bat.

Kingman was limited to just 81 games in 1980 and did three tours on the disabled list. He managed to hit 18 homers.

David Arthur Kingman was born December 28, 1948, in Pendleton, Oregon. His father, Arthur, worked for United Airlines and was based there from 1943-51. He was transferred to a job in Denver in 1951. By 1954, the family moved to Los Angeles for Art's latest assignment.

At eight years old, Dave played 10-inch semi-hardball (mainly as a pitcher and sometimes at first base) in a park recreation league in Hawthorne, in the south bay area of Los Angeles.

During Little League tryouts when Dave was nine years old, the league thought he should play with the 10-11-12-year-olds after he fouled two pitches off and hit two out of the park. They only allowed four pitches.

During his teenage years, Kingman lived in Mt. Prospect in northwest suburban Chicago, where he starred in basketball at Prospect High School. He was named to the All-Area basketball team as a starting center and forward for the Knights in 1967. He was a wide receiver and a safety on the high school football team.

As a high school pitcher, Kingman threw a no-hitter against Niles North High School on April 6, 1967. He pitched a two-hitter in his final high school game and smashed four home runs.

Kingman, who hit a 500-foot home run in high school, was drafted by the Seattle Pilots in 1967 but decided not to sign a contract. He was drafted once again in 1968 by the California Angels, but turned down a $50,000 offer to sign. He was drafted again by the Baltimore Orioles in a special phase draft in 1968 before declining to sign.

Kingman attended Harper Junior College in Palatine, Illinois, in 1968 before beginning his career at the University of Southern California as a sophomore in 1969. He finished 11-4 as a pitcher for the Trojans in '69. In 1970 he was switched to the outfield and slugged nine home runs while batting .355 in 32 games (121 at-bats).

"I've always wanted to be a pitcher, because pitching is really the center of all the action," Kingman said initially. "To me, playing the outfield was like going out to the pasture."

Kingman had fanned 88 batters in 85 innings as a USC sophomore and had hit four homers in only 32 at-bats.

USC coach Rod Dedeaux insisted on performing what he called "The Great Experiment." He converted Kingman into a right fielder to take greater advantage of his bat.

In February, 1970 the Trojans played a three-game series against the Dodgers at Dodger Stadium. Each game drew about 20,000 fans. In the first game on February 13, Kingman hit a home run off Joe Moeller. In the second game on February 15, he went three for three with two doubles, two RBIs and one run scored. In the third game, Kingman hit three doubles off Alan Foster.

In USC's 13th game of the 1970 season, Kingman collided with a teammate and suffered a broken arm and torn ligaments in one leg. He had been hitting .533, but missed 30 games in the seven weeks he was out and returned April 20.

Kingman helped lead USC to the NCAA championship in 1970 with a record of 51-13-1.

He was the San Francisco Giants' No. 1 selection of the June 1970 free agent player draft. This time he finally signed with the Giants and reported to their AA Amarillo team on July 2.

Where Have You Gone?

PETE LaCOCK

Pete LaCock is the son of popular game show host Peter Marshall, but he made a name for himself as a decent big-league first baseman with the Cubs and the Kansas City Royals from 1972-1980.

A .257 career hitter over nine major league seasons, LaCock was the American Association MVP in 1974 after hitting .327 with 23 homers and 91 runs batted in. His best major league season was with the Royals, when he hit .364 in the 1978 American League Championship Series and .295 during the regular season.

Since retiring, LaCock has run in marathons and has competed in triathlons. He has also served as the hitting coach of professional minor league teams, including the Lake County Fielders in 2011. In 2012, he joined the Cronulla Sutherland Baseball Club in Australia.

Born Ralph Pierre LaCock on January 17, 1952, in Burbank, California, the left-handed hitter was a first-round selection of the Cubs (20th overall) in the June, 1970, amateur free agent draft.

The six-foot, three-inch, 210-pound LaCock did not receive signif-icant playing time with the Cubs until 1975, when he batted .229 with six home runs in 106 games.

"Probably one of my biggest memories with the Cubs was the first time I went to hit in batting practice," said LaCock. "I just got brought

Brace Photo

23 · PETE LaCOCK · 1B
Years with Cubs: 1972-76

**Hit 6 HR and had 30 RBI in 1975 • Totaled 15 HR and 73 RBI in 263
games with Cubs**

up from Double A and I was rushed. They already had a uniform for me with my name on it and bats with my name on it. They had just told me I was coming up the night before.

"I remember at that time the locker room at Wrigley for the Cubs was down the left field line. I came out for batting practice and the place was packed. It was just people there watching batting practice. Somebody had written an article about me in the paper that day, so when I came out to hit, everybody looked at me. Then when I got in the batter's box, the one thing that I thought about was the fact that Babe Ruth stood where I was standing [in the 1933 All-Star Game]. It was almost overwhelming. The first pitch I hit went out of the stadium, and the fans went crazy. I will never forget that. Wrigley Field is the greatest place I can imagine being, baseball-wise," he said.

LaCock also will never forget how well the veteran stars on the Cubs treated him when he first arrived in Chicago.

"Guys like Billy Williams and Don Kessinger and Glenn Beckert and Joe Pepitone," said LaCock. "That really made me feel like I was part of the team, even though I was only there [in 1972] for a few weeks because Billy Williams had broken his ankle."

On September 3, 1975, Hall of Fame pitcher Bob Gibson gave up the last hit of his career—a pinch-hit grand slam by LaCock as the Cubs beat the St. Louis Cardinals 11-6.

"That was one of my first big hits at Wrigley Field," said LaCock. "It was the Cardinals series and it was packed. Everything is exciting there. Batting practice is exciting. Once you get to the ballpark, everything is exciting."

LaCock became accustomed to people asking him about his famous father, television star Peter Marshall, who was born Pierre LaCock on March 30, 1927, in Huntington, West Virginia.

"Sometimes it was an advantage and sometimes it was a disadvantage," said LaCock. "It was always an advantage to me because I am very proud of my dad. My dad's sister actually was more famous than my dad. That's [actress] Joanne Dru.

"I grew up with people like Frank Sinatra and Sammy Davis Jr. and other very famous people around my house all the time," said LaCock. "That was a little bit hectic sometimes. I would bring a lot of actors to the ballpark. I enjoyed that. Because the guys who loved baseball, guys like Jamie Farr and Tom Poston and Kevin Costner really enjoyed that.

"It was a different experience for me. Of course, when I was in the minor leagues and not doing well, people would be screaming Hollywood Squares stuff, and say things like, 'Pick so-and-so to block.'

"At least they know who you are," he said with a laugh. "That's good. But I wanted them to know me because I swung the bat well and I hit the baseball hard. Because I really loved baseball."

LaCock enjoyed more outstanding seasons with Kansas City.

The Cubs acquired Gregg Gross from the Royals for Julio Gonzales on December 8, 1976. Then in a three-team trade, the Cubs also received outfielder Jim Dwyer from the New York Mets for LaCock. Then LaCock was sent to Kansas City for Sheldon Mallory, who went to the Mets.

"I always had the ability to play baseball. I wasn't fast. I was just a good solid player who played good defense and hit the ball in clutch situations," said LaCock. "I enjoyed it as much as anybody. I was one of those guys who just liked to come to the ballpark everyday."

In fact, LaCock did not limit his time to roaming around first base at Wrigley Field with the Cubs.

"I used to be at the ballpark at about 6:30 in the morning," he said. "And I would take my dogs out there. They would run the whole stadium. I was a runner then and I still run a lot. I run marathons. So I would get to Wrigley Field and I would run. There wouldn't be anybody there but the grounds crew and a few people. I would let my dogs loose and they would run up into the stands chasing cats and they would just run all over.

"My dogs would come out and jump over the huge tube that held the tarp. They never pooped on it, because I made sure they pooped before they got to the field. I used to live in the towers near the ballpark on Irving Park Road. So I would walk to the ballpark and then I would walk the dogs back to the apartment before the game started. I would come back and be ready for batting practice."

Some of LaCock's most vivid memories with the Cubs occurred when he was not in the lineup.

"I remember the first game I ever played there. Rick Monday was the first batter and we were playing San Diego. All of a sudden [former Padres catcher] Pat Corrales stood up and punched [Monday]. Then a bench-clearing, wild fight ensued. So I am out there fighting people. And I didn't even play," he said.

"Then my second game, Milt Pappas throws eight and two-thirds innings of a perfect game for the Cubs. I think it was a 5-0 game and the 3-2 pitch is called a ball. Then the next batter pops out to give Pappas his no-hitter. I remember going home after that and I hadn't played in either game. I get home and I say to myself: 'Man, I'm exhausted.' And

I hadn't even played. I realized that the big leagues can be mentally exhausting."

During some games when he knew he was not going to play, LaCock said he would wander throughout the tunnels at Wrigley Field that would lead all of the way under the bleachers in the outfield.

"I wanted to see what was out there," he said.

LaCock also recalls the times when the Cubs played all of their home games during the day.

"That made it tough to win there then," he said. "People don't realize how hot it can get during the summer. It was difficult to make the adjustment to nothing but day games after playing night games on the road. And that little dugout they used to have for us was a hot box."

When he did get an opportunity to play in 1972, LaCock tried to make the most of his opportunities. He got three hits in six at-bats that season.

"I got my first hit off Doc Ellis [of the Pirates]. It was a 3-0 ballgame and they were ahead," said LaCock. "I pinch hit for the pitcher and the first pitch went for a base hit. They had thrown the ball in from the outfield and over to Ellis, then he walked it over to me. I just thought that was really nice of him. I ended up being good friends with Doc and Willie Stargell. I see Gene Clines [former Pirate who is now a coach with the Cubs] all the time. There are a lot of good people that I have met through baseball, especially when I played. It was perfect. I had so much fun in the National League."

LaCock stays in touch with several of his former Cubs teammates. "Everyone loves the Cubs," said LaCock. "I was so disappointed when they didn't get to the World Series [in 2003]. We had tickets and I had everything set. I would have bet the farm on it. But Yogi Berra was right, 'It ain't over until it's over.'"

LaCock went on to play in three League Championship Series with the Royals and one World Series in 1980. He hit .333 during the postseason.

"I have been in the playoffs, I have been in the World Series. But nothing compares to the time I had playing at Wrigley Field," said LaCock. "It was the time of my life, being able to play at Wrigley Field."

VANCE LAW

Vance Law signed with the Cubs as a free agent third baseman in 1988 and earned his first All-Star game berth.

A pinched nerve limited him in 1989 when the Cubs captured the division title.

The son of former Pittsburgh Pirates pitcher Vern Law, Vance served as the head baseball coach at Brigham Young University for 13 years.

"I had a chance to coach my oldest son. Tim just graduated from BYU this past year," said Law in 2004. "I have another one named Andrew who is coming into BYU as a shortstop from high school. I have a daughter named Natalie who is in between those two. She is the one who had some health issues when she was four years old when I was playing in Montreal. She is now 21. I also have a 14-year-old son named Adam and a 12-year-old daughter named Sarah.

"My wife and I are watching baseball and softball games nearly every night of the week."

Law was drafted by Pittsburgh in 1978, traded to the Chicago White Sox in March 1982 and became the Sox' regular third baseman in 1983.

Brace Photo

2 · VANCE LAW · 3B
Years with Cubs: 1988-89

All-Star in 1988 • Hit 11 HR and had career highs in batting average (.293), hits (163) and RBI (78) in 1988 • Played in 1989 NLCS • Totaled 18 HR and 120 RBI in 281 games with Cubs

He hit 17 homers in 1984 but then was traded to Montreal for Bob James.

His stint with the Cubs was a career highlight for Law.

"Two of the best years of my baseball career were spent in Chicago. There is no greater place to play the game than at Wrigley Field," he said.

"I only wish that I could have been there longer. It was a wonderful experience. One of the things that I didn't appreciate as much as a player as I do now is...I wish I had interacted more with the fans. I was so involved with my own career that I didn't have a chance to really interact with the fans.

"I felt like I had a real good relationship with many of them, particularly the ones who were regulars behind the third base dugout. I got to speak to a lot of those people. But I wish I had spent a little more time signing autographs and doing those kinds of things. I know how important that is to a fan. And, frankly, I must say that I miss being sought after the way I was back then."

Vern Law was a key to the Pirates winning the 1960 World Series. He captured the National League Cy Young Award with a 20-9 record and a league-high 18 complete games. He won the first and fourth games of that World Series against the Yankees and had a no-decision in Game 7, won by Pittsburgh when Bill Mazeroski belted the famous ninth-inning home run.

Vern and his wife, VaNita, had six children: Veldon, Veryl, Vaughn, Varlin, VaLynda, and Vance.

"I think that is something that caused me to think that this was something that I wanted to do," said Vance. "I used to hang out at the old Forbes Field and at that time there were never any insurance issues. So a couple of my older brothers and I got to shag fly balls during batting practice. When the gates opened, we had to go sit in the stands.

"But that was a lot of fun going to the ballpark and brushing shoulders with Roberto Clemente and Willie Stargell and Manny Sanguillen. Those last two guys became teammates of mine when I came up with the Pirates. That was kind of interesting, being able to play right alongside your childhood idols. My first game was at second base and Willie Stargell was playing first base for the Pirates at that time. This was the guy that I really looked up to since I was about 11 years old when he joined the Pirates.

"I think I was able to adjust to the game of baseball because of my dad," said Law in 2004. "I remember my dad being gone on road trips and things like that. So when I became a player and had a family of my own, it was not too big of an adjustment. I knew that was the way a baseball life is. I think some guys who have never experienced that...that really comes as a shock, as far as how much time is spent away from their family.

"Certainly, I could not have had a career like I had without a very supportive and loving wife. Sharon has supported me through it all and continues to do so even with me at the collegiate level."

Vance said he also gained some early insight into the unwritten rules of the game of baseball.

"I used to eavesdrop when my dad and some of his teammates would talk about brushing guys back and how that was just the nature of the game," he said. "Now it seems like if you throw the ball two inches in off the plate, people get all upset about that. There are great stories of knocking people down that my dad tells, and it is almost expected when that happens."

Born Vance Aaron Law on October 1, 1956, in Boise, Idaho, he was drafted in the 38th round of the 1978 amateur draft by the Pirates.

"The Pirates were my favorite team growing up. I followed the Pirates and I still follow the Pirates, because that is something from my childhood memories," said Law.

"I heard later that it was done as a favor to my dad and I took that the wrong way. Because I thought my dad had called the Pirates and said: 'Hey, give my son a chance.'

"But I came to find out that he never made a phone call. The Pirates just knew I was playing out here. And I guess just out of respect they gave me an opportunity. And that's all I wanted and needed. I tried to make the most of it."

Law was traded to the White Sox on March 21, 1982 with Ernie Camacho for Ross Baumgarten and Butch Edge.

"I was with the White Sox for three years and that was a great experience, playing on the other side of town," said Law. "Chicago is just a great city. Whether you are a Cubs fan or a Sox fan, the loyalties run very deep there. Mr. [Jerry] Reinsdorf and Mr. [Eddie] Einhorn were wonderful. And I enjoyed playing for Tony La Russa. That was kind of my start in the major leagues, even though I came

up with the Pirates for a short time. The opportunity to really play
didn't happen until I was traded to the White Sox."

On May 8 and 9, 1984, against the Milwaukee Brewers, Law
played all 25 innings of the longest game in American League history, establishing the AL record for the longest errorless game by a
third baseman.

"That was spread over two days because we had a 1 a.m. curfew
and we were in the 17th or 18th inning when they called that [May
8]," said Law.

"We resumed that game at six o'clock the next night. I remember that Tom Seaver won that game. He had come in and pitched the
last four or five innings. Then he started the regularly scheduled
game that started at about nine o'clock. He went about five innings
and he ended up getting two wins that day.

"It was a real interesting game because the Brewers went ahead
of us in about the 16th inning by three runs. Then Harold Baines
hit a three-run home run to tie it. Then he ended up hitting a game-
winning homer in the 25th inning to win it. I kept my meager nine-
or 10-game hitting streak going with a one-for-10. I got a hit in my
first at-bat, then went 0 for nine from then on."

On December 7, 1984, Law was dealt to Montreal for Bob
James.

"I went to Montreal for three years and I played with a great ball
club up there," said Law. "It was certainly a different environment
than what I had grown accustomed to there in Chicago. Montreal
was really a hockey town, and we were on the back page of the sports
page. As players, we felt there wasn't a whole lot of interest in what
was going on, other than opening day. Then attendance dwindled
down to 6,000 or 7,000, instead of 45,000 that was there for the
opener.

"We had a great team; we were in the race a couple of those
years. That is where I first played with Andre Dawson. Then he
signed in 1987 with the Cubs, and I was fortunate enough to kind
of be reunited with him in 1988 and '89. I made some great friend-
ships up there in Montreal with teammates like Tim Raines and Tim
Wallach and Terry Francona."

The Cubs signed Law as a free agent on December 14, 1987.

"I had my best full season with the Cubs in 1988, when I had a
chance to play with five of my teammates in the All-Star Game that

year. Then in '89 the pinched nerve in my neck caused me to alter some things in my swing. I really couldn't face the pitcher very well and I had to really open up my stance in order to see. I probably should have just gone on the disabled list. But I had never been on the DL and I just wanted to tough it out. I kind of kept it to myself and eventually it caught up to me. I got off to just a terrible start.

"By the time I started playing well—hitting about .350 in the month of July—the Cubs brought in Luis Salazar for the stretch run. So I didn't play nearly as much toward the end of that 1989 season as I wanted. But they felt that was the move that would help get them over the top. Salazar did have a couple of big games where it did help us. It was nice to be on another division-clinching team. I only wish we had played a little bit better in the playoffs and given the Cubs fans a little bit more to cheer about.

"I felt that because of the year I had in '88 that I would duplicate that year. And I felt like I was starting to turn things around and playing real well again when the move was made. But that's water under the bridge. We ended up winning and the move seemed to work for the Cubs."

Law was a .257 career hitter who played every infield position and was even deployed as a relief pitcher six times in the National League and once in the American League.

"There is no question that third base was my best position," said Law. "I absolutely thought I shined at third base. I remember getting off to a slow start the year I was signed with the Cubs in '88 during spring training. Don Zimmer [then the Cubs' manager] pulled me into the office and said: 'Hey, I don't care if you go 0 for 50 here in spring training. You're still going to be the opening day third baseman. Just relax.'

"That's what I needed to hear. I played well after that in spring training, then got off to a great start during the season. I started the season with a 17- or 18-game hitting streak. I never really experienced a bad slump during the season in '88. I probably only went hitless in no more than three games in a row."

On May 11, 1988, six big-league games went into extra innings, tying the one-day Major League record.

The Mets beat the Astros 9-8 in 10 innings; the Pirates beat the Dodgers 2-1 in 11; the Phillies beat the Reds 4-3 in 11; the Cubs beat the Padres 1-0 on Law's 10th-inning squeeze bunt; the Giants beat the Cardinals 5-4 on Kevin Mitchell's home run in the 16th;

and the Indians beat the Angels 4-3 on Bryan Harvey's 13th-inning balk.

The Cubs released Law on January 2, 1990. He signed with the Oakland A's on January 7, 1991, and was released at the end of that season.

Law served as head baseball coach at Brigham Young for 12 seasons, until his contract was not renewed before the 2012 season. He amassed a career record of 397-347-2 while coaching at his alma mater. He guided BYU to the Mountain West Conference championship in 2001, the same year he was named Coach of the Year.

But several mediocre years followed at BYU, and his Cougars lost his final game 17-1 to Gonzaga.

"I'm really grateful for the opportunity to coach these young men. That's really the bottom line," Law told the media afterwards. "This day was for those [six] seniors, it wasn't about me. It isn't about the situation I've found myself in. It's really about those guys.

"It was made clear....nothing less than making it into the [NCAA] tournament would matter. I knew that going in."

Law was replaced for the 2012 season by Mike Littlewood.

Where Have You Gone?

ED LYNCH

The first former Cubs player to become the club's general manager since Charlie Grimm (1934-1938, 1949-1950), Ed Lynch played professionally from 1977-1988, pitching in 248 major league games with the New York Mets (1980-1986) and the Cubs (1986-87).

As a pitcher the six-foot, five-inch right-hander finished his career with a 47-54 record, eight saves and a 4.00 earned run average, playing most of his career with the Mets. In 1986 with the Cubs, Lynch was 7-5 with a 3.79 ERA as both a starter and reliever after being acquired from the Mets on June 30. He never led any league in a single statistic during his professional career and had only four winning seasons.

When he played for the Mets, Lynch was known for his "big-league talk" when he was interviewed by sportswriters from the *New York Times.* For instance, he was once quoted as saying: "The bases were drunk, and I painted the black with my best yakker. But blue squeezed me, and I went full. I came back with my heater, but the stick flares one the other way and chalk flies for two bases. Three earnies! Next thing I know, skipper hooks me and I'm sipping suds with the clubby."

Born February 25, 1956, Lynch was the captain of his baseball and basketball teams at Columbus High School in Miami. He was 6-1 with a 2.32 ERA as South Carolina finished second in the College World

AP/WWP

37 · ED LYNCH · P
Years with Cubs: 1986-87

Went 7-5 with 3.79 ERA and three CG after midseason acquisition in 1986 • Pitched in 81 games with 21 starts and four saves with Cubs

Series in 1977. Lynch then was selected in the 22nd round of the 1977 amateur draft by Texas.

He earned a bachelor's degree in finance from the University of South Carolina. He also has a master's degree in business administration from the University of Miami.

Lynch was named general manager of the Cubs on October 10, 1994. He was promoted to vice president/general manager on October 26, 1998.

During his tenure as the Cubs' general manager, the club had a pair of plus-.500 campaigns and earned a playoff berth in 1998 as the National League's wild card team—just their third postseason appearance since World War II. In 1998, Lynch tied for third place in *The Sporting News'* Executive of the Year voting.

Lynch came to the Cubs after spending one year as the Mets' special assistant to executive vice president of baseball operations Joe McIlvaine. He also served as the San Diego Padres' director of minor leagues from November 1990-September 1993.

On July 18, 2000, the Cubs announced that Lynch had resigned his title as the club's vice president/general manager, effective immediately.

Lynch had been offered and accepted another position within the organization.

The team also announced that Andy MacPhail would assume the role and responsibilities of the general manager's position, at least through the conclusion of the 2001 season.

MacPhail was named the Cubs' president and chief executive officer on September 9, 1994. He joined the Cubs after serving as the executive vice president/general manager of the Minnesota Twins (November 1986-September 1994). Under his guidance, the Twins won World Series championships in 1987 and 1991.

On doing both jobs, MacPhail said: "I'm going to get it done or it will kill me. ... If I don't get it done, they will have only one person to look at, not two people."

In November 1998, the Cubs extended Lynch's contract through the 2001 season. At the time, MacPhail said Lynch's leadership during the 1997 season—when the Cubs finished 68-94—was a significant factor in the team's decision.

The Cubs were 39-53, 14 1/2 games behind St. Louis in the NL Central, when Lynch resigned in July of 2000.

"I would like to apologize to the fans. I'm sorry I was not able to bring a winner to the greatest fans in baseball," Lynch said after the announcement. "I am glad we gave them a good run in 1998," the year the Cubs made the playoffs as a wild card team.

Lynch offered his resignation two months earlier, but MacPhail said the offer came when he had to deal with a brawl in the stands at Wrigley Field between Cubs fans and Los Angeles Dodgers players.

So, MacPhail said, he put off a decision until after the All-Star break.

"It was a development that evolved over time," MacPhail said. "It was easy to see his frustration. I was frustrated along with him. So it really wasn't a surprise."

The Cubs made the playoffs in 1998 as the NL wild card by riding Sammy Sosa's phenomenal 66-homer season, the pitching of Kerry Wood and the leadership of veterans like Gary Gaetti, Mickey Morandini and Rod Beck.

The Cubs decided to stick with those veterans the next season. And even with Wood out for the season following elbow surgery, the Cubs rolled to a 32-24 start in early June. Then came a startling collapse.

They won only 35 games the final four months of 1999. And in 2000, despite new manager Don Baylor and the acquisition of Eric Young, Damon Buford, Ismael Valdes, Joe Girardi and Ricky Gutierrez; the Cubs were 14 1/2 games behind St. Louis in the NL Central.

"I don't know when the downfall began," Lynch said. "Coming off the '98 season we felt we had players who could continue to be productive. And they were in June. We had the fifth best record in baseball. Then the bottom just fell out, but I didn't view that as the beginning of the end."

Lynch termed the Cubs' dismal play for his last year "an equal opportunity failure in a lot of ways." The relief pitching, the starting rotation and the hitting never seemed to be in sync. If one was good, the other was awful.

"We just never clicked. Across the board at one time or the other we've had problems in every facet of the game," Lynch said, adding he couldn't fire a manager like Jim Riggleman and not hold himself accountable, as well.

"For me to do anything different would be hypocritical," he said. He said the Sosa situation, in which the star outfielder was almost traded during a two-week stretch of constant rumors, did not affect his decision to resign.

"Sammy and my decision are totally separate," he said.

Since his days playing for the Cubs, Lynch has lived in Arizona and helped the Cubs in another capacity.

"I am a professional scout. I go out and see other clubs and their upper-minor league players," said Lynch in 2004. "I help [current Cubs general manager] Jim Hendry when he needs to make a trade or make a claim on waivers or sign free agents. I see several hundred players, and that is the information Jim uses along with some of the other information from other scouts. The name of the game is information, and that is basically what the scouts do. They provide information to the general manager and help him make informed decisions."

The Cubs were up and down during his tenure. But after being away from the GM position a few years, Lynch tried to objectively assess his complete body of work.

"We didn't inherit a lot when Andy [MacPhail] and I came in here in 1994," he said. "When you look at our lineup back in those days, it is 100 percent different now. We took the time to try to build the organization from the bottom up. We made some pretty good draft picks and some pretty good trades. But Jim Hendry has just done a fabulous job since taking over. In my opinion, I don't think any other GM in the league has done as good a job as he has. If I was voting, I certainly would vote for Jim Hendry as Executive of the Year. And Dusty [Baker] has done a super job. To me, he is the National League Manager of the Year. I don't see anyone else close."

Lynch was involved in scouting the Florida Marlins before the 2003 National League Championship Series against the Cubs and has also worked as a scout within the Toronto Blue Jays' organization.

"I was watching Florida since September 16 [2003]," said Lynch. "I saw them in Philadelphia, then in Atlanta for four games and then six in Miami, and then in the playoffs. I was responsible for [watching] the pitchers. I try to give [Cubs first base coach] Sonny Jackson and Dusty Baker and [hitting coach] Gary Matthews an idea of how I think their pitchers are going to attack our hitters. It's pretty standard stuff, but if there is an edge there, you hope to find it."

KEITH MORELAND

On Feb. 16, 2011, WGN Radio announced that Keith Moreland would be the new Cubs color analyst to replace Ron Santo in the broadcast booth. After the Dec. 3, 2010, passing of Santo, Moreland fairly seamlessly stepped in with veteran play-by-play voice Pat Hughes.

Moreland recognized the popularity and fan following that Santo had garnered and immediately said that it was not his intent to try to replace Santo as a personality.

The leading hitter for the Cubs in 1983, Moreland, the right fielder, was remarkably versatile, considering his lack of speed.

Moreland was signed originally as a third baseman and became a catcher in 1977 with the Philadelphia Phillies. After receiving just part-time duty with the Phillies, he was dealt to the Cubs and shifted to the outfield. His potent bat kept him in the lineup. He hit .302 in 1983 and .307 with 14 homers and 106 RBI in 1985.

Moreland was shifted back to third base in 1987 in an attempt to replace Ron Cey, but he struggled defensively. He did manage to hit a career-high 27 home runs that season. Moreland was traded to San Diego in 1988 for veteran relief ace Goose Gossage. In 1989, it was on to Detroit for Moreland, before being dealt to Baltimore in midseason because the Orioles were contending.

Brace Photo

6 · KEITH MORELAND · OF
Years with Cubs: 1982-87

Had career-high 27 HR in 1988 • Ranked fourth in NL with 106 RBI and ninth with 180 hits in 1985 • Hit .333 with two RBI in 1984 NLCS • Totaled 100 HR and 491 RBI with Cubs

Moreland worked for 16 years for the Longhorn Sports Network, doing the color commentary for the University of Texas football and baseball teams' games.

Following retirement from baseball, Moreland moved to Austin, Texas, and earned his college degree at the university.

Moreland joined the Cubs on December 8, 1981. A trade during the winter meetings sent Philadelphia pitchers Dickie Noles and Dan Larsen and Moreland to the Cubs in exchange for starter Mike Krukow.

Moreland had hit .333 for the Phillies in the 1980 World Series, going four for 12. During the 1980 season, he batted .314 in 62 games. He hit his first big-league homer off Cincinnati's Tom Seaver on May 21, 1980.

Born May 2, 1954, in Dallas, Bobby Keith Moreland graduated from R.L. Turner High School in Dallas in 1972. He lettered in baseball, football and basketball in high school, before attending the University of Texas, where the six-foot 210-pounder played football and baseball. As a sophomore Moreland was a starting defensive back for legendary Longhorns coach Darryl Royal. Moreland broke his wrist during the opening game of his senior year against Oklahoma.

On the Texas baseball team, Moreland was an All-America third baseman and was a member of the Longhorns' 1975 NCAA championship team.

He immediately began paying dividends for the Cubs on May 7, 1982, when Moreland blasted two home runs and drove in seven runs during a 12-6 rout of the Phillies.

Former Cubs left fielder Gary Matthews, who joined the team in 1983, was impressed with the ability of Moreland.

"I don't think I have ever seen a better hitter at the plate when the game is on the line than Keith Moreland," said Matthews. "He is a real student of the game and squeezes every bit of performance out of the talent he has. He really works at being a special type of 'gamer.' Keith is not exactly fast as a gazelle out there, but he seems to get the job done at all times."

The Cubs emerged from humble beginnings in 1983 after finishing a dismal fifth (71-91). The 1984 Cubs had lost a club-record 11 straight exhibition games and finished with a 7-20 preseason mark, the worst in the majors.

Then on March 27, 1984, the Cubs acquired Matthews and center fielder Bobby Dernier from the Phillies.

As a member of the Phillies, Matthews was dubbed "Sarge" by former teammate Pete Rose when Philadelphia captured the World Series title.

The Cubs only had to give up 37-year-old reliever Bill Campbell and minor league catcher Mike Diaz to acquire Matthews and Dernier.

But Moreland, who had batted a career-high .306 in 1983, became disconsolate immediately after the big trade. That was because the trade meant left handed-hitting Mel Hall would platoon with Moreland in right field. Since there are considerably more right-handed pitchers than lefties, Moreland only had a chance to start about 15 to 20 percent of the time.

Moreland repeatedly entreated the Cubs to trade him during this period of turmoil, and he beefed publicly about the manner in which he was treated.

Around the clubhouse, Moreland sang: "Please release me, let me go."

Moreland finally said: "I have nothing against the new players on the team. Matthews and Dernier are good players. I just want to play, too. If that means going to another ball club, well, that's how badly I want to play."

Hall was eventually traded to the Cleveland Indians in a controversial trade on June 13, 1984. Rookie outfield sensation Joe Carter and two minor leaguers also packed their bags for Cleveland in exchange for pitchers Rick Sutcliffe and George Frazier and catcher Ron Hassey.

For starters, the Cubs' front office neglected to obtain waivers on Hall and Carter, meaning those two players were unable to play for the Indians for a five-day clearance period.

Hall, facing the prospect of returning to the Cubs if another team had claimed him on waivers, blasted the Cubs organization for dealing him.

"Who is Rick Sutcliffe?" ranted Hall in a familiar refrain. "I hope I face him sometime."

Meanwhile, Sutcliffe went on to win the National League Cy Young Award. Bringing a 4-5 record with him from Cleveland, Sutcliffe was 16-1 with the Cubs, including a club-record 14 straight regular-season wins.

Moreland seemed to be revitalized after Hall was sent packing for Cleveland. He wound up the '84 season with 16 home runs and 80 runs batted in. He was named NL Player of the Month in August when he batted .360 with five homers and 32 RBIs.

On August 7, 1984, the Cubs swept a pair of games from the visiting New York Mets. Sutcliffe beat Ron Darling in the opener, thanks to a six-run fifth inning. Moreland hit a three-run homer and Cey belted a two-run shot. In the second game of the doubleheader, the Cubs mounted a five-run fourth inning to give reliever Tim Stoddard the win and Lee Smith picked up his 25th save.

On the next day, the Cubs completed a four-game sweep of the Mets with a 7-6 victory. Moreland led the way with three hits and four runs batted in. The contest featured a beanball incident. When Dernier was plunked by a pitch, Mets manager Davey Johnson was tossed from the game. When the Cubs retaliated by having Lee Smith throw behind George Foster, manager Jim Frey got the thumb.

The Mets rebounded from that series sweep when Dwight Gooden tossed a one-hitter against the Cubs on September 7, 1984. Moreland got the only hit, a slow roller down the third base line in the fifth inning.

Ryne Sandberg, then 24, was the NL Most Valuable Player in 1984, hitting .314 with a league-high 114 runs scored, 36 doubles, 19 homers and a .520 slugging percentage.

The Cubs captured the division title behind Sutcliffe's masterful two-hitter in Pittsburgh on September 24, 1984. Sutcliffe struck out nine and walked none as the Cubs defeated the Pirates 4-1.

The San Diego Padres ended the Cubs' dream of playing in the World Series for the first time in 39 years.

The Cubs struggled because of major injuries the next few seasons. But on June 3, 1987, they routed the Houston Astros 22-7 at Wrigley Field. The game featured a major league-tying three grand slams. Moreland and Brian Dayett connected for the Cubs. And Houston's Billy Hatcher, a former Cub, hit a grand slam for the Astros.

On February 12, 1988, Moreland was sent to the Padres for Gossage. The Tigers traded pitcher Walt Terrell to San Diego for Moreland and third baseman Chris Brown on October 28, 1988.

As Moreland prepared to work his first regular-season Cubs broadcast, he compared the experience to breaking into the major leagues as a player with the Phillies in 1980.

"They are close," said Moreland. "I can remember that I was called to the big leagues a couple of times before I actually made a big league roster out of spring training. And when that happened that first time, you were sort of, 'Yeah, I'm all right with this.' Then, the day came. Then you sort of get there. Well, it is sort of the same thing for this. I've had some opportunities to do some substituting [for the late Ron Santo on WGN Radio]. I worked with such great people here. But this is a little different.

"I can just tell this is going to be a little different than a normal, 'Hey, let's just broadcast.'"

Moreland, who was a member of the 1984 Cubs team that lost 11 straight spring training games but went on to capture the division title, felt the 2011 Cubs squad would surprise observers.

"We won 7 spring training games," said Moreland. "There are two things that we didn't have in '84 that this team DOES have. They have pretty good starting pitching and a great bullpen. Anytime you've got good pitching, you've got a chance. Now it's about putting those tallies on the board, and I think that will be the key to the season."

Of course, the 2011 season proved to be yet another disappointing year for Cubs fans.

*****

As Moreland prepared to work his first regular-season Cubs broadcast, he compared the experience to breaking into the major leagues as a player with the Phillies in 1980.

"They are close," said Moreland. "I can remember that I was called to the big leagues a couple of times before I actually made a big league roster out of spring training. And when that happened that first time, you were sort of, 'Yeah, I'm all right with this.' Then, the day came. Then you sort of get there. Well, it is sort of the same thing for this. I've had some opportunities to do some substituting [for the late Ron Santo on WGN Radio]. I worked with such great people here. But this is a little different.

"I can just tell this is going to be a little different than a normal, 'Hey, let's just broadcast.'"

Moreland, who was a member of the 1984 Cubs team that lost 11 straight spring training games but went on to capture the division title, felt the 2011 Cubs squad would surprise observers.

"We won 7 spring training games," said Moreland. "There are two things that we didn't have in '84 that this team DOES have. They have pretty good starting pitching and a great bullpen. Anytime you've got good pitching, you've got a chance. Now it's about putting those tallies on the board, and I think that will be the key to the season."

Of course, the 2011 season proved to be yet another disappointing year for Cubs fans.

DICKIE NOLES

Dickie Noles pitched in the big leagues for 11 years with the Cubs, Phillies, Rangers, Indians, Tigers and Orioles.

He was a member of the 1980 World Series champion Phillies. Noles is admittedly a recovering alcoholic and has been an active speaker on the prevention of drug and alcohol use since his recovery began on April 9, 1983.

Noles has attended and taught many workshops and seminars on substance abuse, and is recognized nationally as a motivational speaker. Each year he speaks to thousands of youth on the dangers of alcohol and other drugs.

Noles was hired full-time by the Phillies as an employee assistance counselor, working with all major and minor league players, coaches and office personnel. He also travels to each of the Phillies' minor league teams to educate young players on substance abuse.

"I have been doing this for about 10 years," said Noles in 2004. "I handle all of the personal problems of the players. Of course, I do a lot of community work. I have my own program designed for troubled kids and emotionally disturbed youngsters. So I stay pretty busy."

Born November 19, 1956, in Charlotte, North Carolina, Dickie Ray Noles was selected by the Phillies on June 3, 1975, in the fourth round

Brace Photo

48 · DICKIE NOLES · P
Years with Cubs: 1982-84, 1987

**Won career-high 10 games and made 30 starts in 1982 •
Totaled 21 wins and 127 appearances with Cubs**

of the amateur draft. He broke into the big leagues on July 5, 1979. He went 3-4 with a 3.80 earned run average that season as a starter in 14 games. He was 1-4 in 1980, splitting his time as a starter and reliever.

After spending seven seasons in the Phillies organization, he was traded with Dan Larson and Keith Moreland to the Chicago Cubs for Mike Krukow and cash on December 8, 1981.

"It's funny because Bobby Dernier and I were at a Phillies reunion recently," said Noles at the 2004 Chicago Cubs Fans Convention.

"We had the 1980 Phillies team honored back in Philadelphia because we were the world champs. The only one in Phillies history. They went around the room and asked us all to talk about ourselves. Bobby Dernier stood up and mentioned the Phillies and mentioned the Cubs. I followed 'Bobby D' and said: 'You know what. Half of me is the Phillies and the other half is the Cubs.' So Bobby jumped up and said: 'I really appreciate that.' Right after that, I got invited to this Cubs Convention. Some of my fondest memories in baseball were here in Chicago. I love Chicago and I loved playing here. I got my first opportunity to start, really, in the big leagues in Chicago in 1982 [career-high 31 starts]. Of course my life fell apart in 1983."

Noles spent six weeks in an alcohol rehabilitation center in 1983 when he was with the Cubs.

"I got my life together the following year. I have so many memories as a Cub," he said.

After several alcohol-related incidents, including an arrest in Cincinnati following a fight in a tavern, and mediocre mound performances, Noles was traded to the Texas Rangers on July 2, 1984, for two minor leaguers. Noles appeared to turn his life around while with Texas. He volunteered for numerous community service functions as a spokesman denouncing the abuse of drugs and alcohol.

The Rangers then sent minor leaguers Tim Henry and Jorge Gomez to the Cubs on December 11, 1984, to complete the trade.

Noles was released by the Rangers on December 20, 1985. He signed with the Cleveland Indians on February 8, 1986. Noles signed as a free agent with the Cubs again on April 6, 1987. He arrived in Chicago with his wife and daughter from their home in Arlington, Texas, immediately after that trade.

Former Phillies manager Dallas Green was the Cubs' general manager at this point, and he had a special place in his heart for Noles and his ongoing problems with alcohol off the field.

"I think you know the special feeling we have for Dickie, and we still think he can compete," said Green. "Dickie didn't have a job."

"Noles has a good arm, and I remember seeing him with Texas and with the Phillies," said Gene Michael, the Cubs' manager in 1987 after Jim Frey was fired. "He's always been a good competitor. We need more arms in camp anyway. He gives us 18 pitchers. A lot of teams have 22 or 23 in camp."

Asked if he felt Noles could make the last-place Cubs team, Michael replied: "Yeah, you're darn right. We're open in the pitching and outfield positions."

Noles quickly earned the respect of his Cubs teammates in 1987.

A bench-clearing melee unfolded in the eighth inning of a game against the Expos, when Noles hit Montreal's Andres "the Cat" Galarraga with a pitch. Noles had hit two Expos in the seventh inning the previous night, including Galarraga during a relief stint.

The first night, Galarraga had simply glared menacingly at Noles after being plunked. The following night, The Cat took action, charging the mound and swinging like a madman before pouncing on Noles.

The Olympic Stadium fight was declared a draw, but the Expos held on for a 5-4 victory in the main event in front of 13,777 spectators.

The Cubs pulled to within a run on Rafael Palmeiro's two-run pinch-hit homer in the ninth. Keith Moreland, who stranded seven runners (six in scoring position), popped up with the bases loaded to end the game.

Noles, who was ejected from the game along with Galarraga, injured his right wrist.

"That fight was scary," said Palmeiro, a rookie in 1987 and involved in his first major league mixer. "You have to just go in there and grab somebody, and hopefully nobody gets you.

"I was right in there with [Herm] Winningham. I just told him: 'Hey, cool out. We don't want anybody to get hurt out here.' It's dangerous out there. There's guys out there just trying to get the first person they can. They hit Andre [Dawson] earlier in the game."

Gene Michael said he had no problem with the fisticuffs. "They hit Dawson," he said. "That's part of the game. I don't mind it. Dickie is a tough competitor."

A second look at the X-rays of Noles's right wrist two days later revealed a broken bone, so the Cubs placed the veteran right-hander on the 21-day disabled list and called up reliever Mark Leonette from Triple-A Iowa.

Noles said he hurt his wrist when plate umpire Joe West accidentally forced him to the ground trying to break up the bench-clearing brawl.

"I keep in touch with Warren Brusstar, Jody Davis, Keith Moreland and Ferguson Jenkins. I think my wife loves Fergie more than me," said Noles in 2004. "All of these people were instrumental in me turning my life around. They really cared about me and helped me come back here in '87. I know we finished last that season, but to see Andre Dawson have an MVP season was something. Why that guy is not in the Hall of Fame, I have no idea."

Noles had a 4-2 record and 3.50 record with the Cubs in 1987, but he was sent to the Detroit Tigers on September 22, 1987, as part of a conditional trade. As it turned out, Noles was the player to be named later in that deal, and returned to the Cubs on October 23, 1987.

That transaction caused quite a bit of controversy.

The office of then baseball commissioner Peter Ueberroth contacted Green and Detroit Tigers president Jim Campbell regarding the investigation of the suspicious late-season trade involving Noles.

"Both the Cubs and the Tigers were requested to submit a written explanation of their thought processes in making the trade," said Ned Colletti, then the Cubs' media relations director.

The Cubs had dealt Noles to the Tigers during Detroit's September pennant drive with the Toronto Blue Jays. The Cubs were to be compensated by the ubiquitous "player to be named." After Noles notched two saves to help the Tigers win the American League East, he was traded back to the Cubs a month later as the "player to be named." In essence, the Cubs loaned Noles to the Tigers.

"We're still collecting information about it. We're reviewing the situation," Bill Murray, an administrator in the commissioner's office, said from New York at the time. "After we get everything in, we will release something on it. Maybe by the end of the week, we will know something. There is a prohibition against lending players to another organization."

An unnamed source working closely with the investigation said: "The ramifications of this investigation could be very serious for any club official involved in this. We could be talking about fines and a possible dismissal.

"The Players' Association, for example, could file a grievance on behalf of the Toronto Blue Jays saying that they could have won the AL East if Noles had not been a member of the Tigers. They could file a grievance demanding the difference in a share for a first-place finish and a second-place finish. Same thing with the St. Louis Cardinals. They could argue that they could have beaten the Blue Jays in the World Series instead of losing to Minnesota. This could be very serious and there could be some very hard action."

The perception of unethical doings appeared to be a bigger issue than the practical nature of the deal. The commissioner's office had to determine whether the trade was made with the premeditated intent to return Noles to the Cubs.

"It does not look real good . . . the whole precept of trading a player for a player to be named later, when the player to be named is that player," said American League President Bobby Brown.

According to the commissioner's office, there had been at least four previous deals made in the major leagues involving a player being dealt for himself, including one involving former Cubs catcher Harry Chiti and the Cleveland Indians in the early '60s.

Detroit general manager Bill Lajoie gave his explanation to the commissioner's office.

"Whoever made the complaint did not consider that this could be a forerunner or the first part of a major transaction," Lajoie said. "There were several other players mentioned originally.

"Due to the time of the year—we were in a pennant race—we didn't want to divulge the other part of the deal because the players were still playing. The Cubs and us are still working on the major portion of the trade."

Lajoie made his remarks just before Green resigned from his Cubs post.

The Tigers reportedly were prepared to trade reliever Willie Hernandez to the Cubs. The Philadelphia Phillies also were going to send infielder Rick Schu to the Cubs. First baseman Leon Durham of the Cubs would have gone to the Phillies. The Tigers would have received an unnamed player from the Phillies.

It is believed the deal fell through when the Phillies hired Woody Woodward to become general manager, and he said he did not want Durham.

"I was very upset that I had to put names in this statement [to the commissioner]," Lajoie said, "because nobody likes to read they're being considered for a trade."

In his 32 days with the Tigers, Noles earned two saves, including one against the second-place Toronto Blue Jays. The two teams played each other seven times in the final 11 days.

Commissioner Ueberroth's office could not determine if the trade was made with the intent of Noles returning to the Cubs.

"I'm surprised it even came up," Lajoie said. "It's probably sour grapes on the part of somebody in Toronto that this whole thing got started."

Noles finished his big-league career on October 15, 1990, after spending the final three seasons with the Baltimore Orioles, New York Yankees and the Phillies.

Where Have You Gone?

ANDY PAFKO

A ndy Pafko, a proud native of Boycefield, Wisconsin, was the starting center fielder on the 1945 Cubs team that won the National League pennant before losing to Detroit in seven games in the World Series.

The versatile Pafko, nicknamed "Handy Andy" during his playing days as a third baseman and outfielder, still lives in the Chicago area.

"I lost my wife about three years ago. But I love Chicago. I made a lot of friends here and it is such a great city, so I stay here," said Pafko in 2004. "Those years go by fast when you get older."

As the 2004 season approached, Pafko wondered aloud: How much longer must Cubs fans wait for another pennant?

The 1945 Cubs finished with a 98-56 record, winning the pennant by three games behind manager Charlie Grimm. Pafko batted .298 with 110 RBIs that year. He says it is difficult to find similarities between the recent Cubs teams and the '45 squad.

"When I played for the Cubs, it was during the war years. So a lot of the great hitters then were in the service. This is a different era. It is hard to compare one era with another. But it is still a great game," Pafko said.

Brace Photo

48 · ANDY PAFKO · OF
Years with Cubs: 1943-51

Five-time All-Star • Had 12 HR and 110 RBI in 1945 • Batted career-best .312 and totaled 26 HR and 101 RBI in 1948 • Hit career-high 36 HR and had 92 RBI in 1950 • Hit .300 or better in three seasons • Had two RBI in 1945 World Series • Totaled 126 HR and 584 RBI with Cubs

After World War II, Pafko put together three .300 seasons with the Cubs. He also hit 36 home runs in 1950.

"We were in a tough race with the Cardinals in '45. We won [the pennant] on the next to last game against Pittsburgh," he recalled. "In fact, I drove in the winning run. I will never forget it. We had a nice party that night. That was the first time I ever tasted champagne. It tasted mighty good."

Pafko was a member of the Cubs organization from 1943-51 and spent 17 years in the majors with a lifetime batting average of .285, 213 homers and 976 RBIs. Yet he never made more than $30,000 a year. He insists he does not feel resentful about that.

"Not at all. I played during a great era of baseball. I was fortunate to play in the World Series for three different teams in my career—the Chicago Cubs, the Brooklyn Dodgers and the Milwaukee Braves. There have been so many great Cubs ballplayers like Ernie Banks, Billy Williams and Ron Santo who never got the chance to play in a World Series. This is tremendous this year. I am so excited for the fans. They have been waiting for this since 1945, so I hope this is the year. If anybody deserves this, it is the wonderful Chicago fans. I am pulling so hard for the Cubs to make it to the World Series. It will bring back a lot of memories."

Pafko enjoyed many memorable games with the Cubs. For instance, on May 31, 1948, the Cubs set a paid attendance record at Wrigley Field with 46,965 fans to watch a doubleheader with the Pirates. The Cubs won the opener, 4-3 behind reliever Bob Rush. Then they lost the night-cap, 4-2 to Elmer Riddle. Pafko ripped five hits, including a home run in each game.

One of the Cubs' most popular players, Pafko was traded to the Dodgers in 1951, much to the dismay of Chicago fans. Pafko teamed with Duke Snider in center and Carl Furillo in right to complete a very formidable outfield for Brooklyn. Pafko's 19 homers and 85 RBIs helped the Dodgers to the pennant in 1952. Brooklyn traded him to the Braves after the 1952 season, moving Jackie Robinson into the vacated left field position for a year. Pafko platooned on Milwaukee's world champions of 1957 and pennant winners of 1958.

With the exception of a few cosmetic changes to the ballpark, Pafko sees little difference between the Wrigley Field he played in when the Cubs drew over a million fans in 1945 and finished with a 49-26 record.

"This park looks the same as it did in the good old days," he said in 2004. "I hope they never move from this park. It's wonderful. They had the outfield roped off then because fans were sitting in the outfield. Then someone got hit in the head out there and folks in the front office said: 'We better do something about that center field.' So as an outfielder you had to be careful out there."

On August 2, 1950, Pafko hit three home runs in the second game of a doubleheader, but the Cubs lost both to the Giants, 11-1 and 8-6. Pafko is one of only a few members of that '45 Cubs team still alive to tell us about it.

The perennial question for all Cubs fans: How long do you think it will be before the Cubs reach the World Series again?

"The years go by and, of course, it has been a long time since 1945," said Pafko in 2004, after watching the Cubs come within five outs of making it to the World Series in 2003 against the eventual world champion Florida Marlins.

"I hope the Cubs can win another one in my lifetime because I am not getting any younger. Dusty Baker has had a good record as a manager. As a matter of fact, Dusty played for me in the minor leagues in 1967. He was in the Braves farm system. I hope he has a good year."

The Cubs' opening day lineup in 1945 had Paul Derringer pitching, Stan Hack at third base, Lennie Merullo at shortstop, Don Johnson at second, Phil Cavarretta at first, Mickey Livingston catching, Hank Sauer in left field, Bill Nicholson in right, and Pafko in center. Few players from that team are still alive.

Pafko remains grateful for the opportunity the Cubs gave him.

On September 24, 1943, a crowd of 314, the smallest in Wrigley Field history, saw Pafko make his Cubs debut. Pafko drove in four runs with a double and a single in three at-bats, as the Cubs beat the Phillies 7-4 in a rain abbreviated five-inning game.

"Well, it was the greatest opportunity I ever had in baseball," he said. "I was just a young kid out of Triple A in 1944. And then in my second full year, I am in the big leagues. That's something I will never, ever forget."

On April 30, 1949, Rocky Nelson hit what was described as an "inside the glove" two-run homer in short left field to transform a 3-1 Cubs lead into a 4-3 St. Louis Cardinals victory. Pafko's apparent catch in center field was ruled a trap by umpire Al Barlick. As Pafko raced in toward the infield holding the ball high in the air, the runners circled the bases to take the lead.

Pafko hit .222 in 24 World Series games. On January 17, 1953, the Boston Braves sold Pafko back to Brooklyn for Roy Hartsfield and $50,000.

MILT PAPPAS

Milt Pappas was born and raised in Detroit, where he starred at Cooley High School. He went 7-0 with a 0.50 earned run average his senior year. He signed with the Baltimore Orioles for $4,000 and advanced to the major leagues after just three games in the minors.

Known as a precise control pitcher, Pappas won 209 games for four teams: Baltimore, Cincinnati, Atlanta and the Chicago Cubs.

He started an All-Star Game and threw a no-hitter with the Cubs during his 17-year career. He never won more than 17 games in any one season, but he recorded between 12-17 victories 13 times, including ten years in a row.

After the 1965 season, the 26-year-old Pappas and two prospects were traded to the Cincinnati Reds for Frank Robinson. Pappas struggled to fit in with the Reds, while Robinson would earn an American League Most Valuable Player award.

"The first time you get traded, that's the toughest. But I tried to put it into perspective. I thought, if I'm being traded for Frank Robinson, that must mean I am pretty good," Pappas said.

"He went over to Baltimore and won the Triple Crown and the Orioles won the World Series in 1966. But the [Cincinnati] fans were just merciless on me. They just booed the living hell out of me. It was

Brace Photo

32 · MILT PAPPAS · P
Years with Cubs: 1970-73

Posted 17-7 record with 2.77 ERA in 1972 • Also had 17 wins with 14 CG in 1971 • Won 51 games and had 112 starts and 31 CG with Cubs

horrible there. I kept saying, 'Hey, I didn't make the trade. Bill DeWitt [Reds boss] made the trade. If you want to boo somebody, boo him. Leave me alone.'"

A World Series championship eluded Pappas during his career. He was traded by the Orioles in 1965, and they won the World Series in 1966. He was dealt by the Reds in '68, and they went to the World Series two years later. With Atlanta he finally made the playoffs in 1969, but they were swept by the surprising New York Mets.

It has been over 40 years (September 2, 1972) since Pappas's no-hitter and near perfect game against the San Diego Padres at Wrigley Field. Home plate umpire Bruce Froemming called a close 3-2 pitch a ball with two outs in the ninth inning to ruin it. Pappas has yet to get over that controversial call.

"That will never go away. Everytime the no-hitter and perfect game comes up... my fat buddy Bruce Froemming is still umpiring. He's still ornery. Nobody likes the guy," said Pappas.

Pappas was able to empathize with former Tigers pitcher Armando Galarraga, who was denied a perfect game by an admitted blown call by first base umpire Jim Joyce on June 3, 2010.

While he believes balls and strikes should remain arbitrary, Pappas feels instant replay should be installed in baseball for plays such as the one that robbed Galarraga of being credited with a perfect game.

Joyce apologized profusely to Galarraga after the game. Pappas said his four decades of anguish toward Froemming would have been more manageable, had Froemming apologized to him.

"Yeah, it would have," Pappas said. "The only problem I have... here you have an umpire [Joyce] right after the ballgame, seeing the review and saying he's sorry. Well, to me that's not good enough. You're right there [on the field], why can't something be done to change it? That's my question, and that's where I think Bud Selig is going to step in...if he's got the guts to do it, which I doubt.

"Here's a situation where I think the instant replay would have been fantastic, to be used in that situation. I don't say that balls and strikes should be scrutinized by the instant replay. But I do think the situation right there is a perfect case where that should have been used, and the call reversed. Do I say it should be used for balls and strikes? No, I don't think so. But in that instance, where you are talking a perfect game, I think it should have been utilized."

Pappas used the Joyce mistake as an opportunity to further disparage Froemming for calling a borderline pitch a ball to ruin his perfect game bid.

"He just passed it off, then years later, he makes the remark: 'Well, I didn't know he had a perfect game,'" said Pappas. "What are you talking about, dummy? Where's your head? He had no idea that nobody had reached first base? And now he's saying he had no idea that a perfect game was going on? This guy is a complete idiot.

"Bruce Froemming had no idea there was a perfect game going on...well, that just now irritates the living hell out of me. Where's your head, man? You don't realize the fact that nobody has touched first base? You didn't realize there was a perfect game going on? Good Lord! Come on. Most umpires will give you the benefit of the doubt in a situation like that."

Pappas made his big-league debut on August 10, 1957 against the New York Yankees in relief. He became a part of the Orioles' starting rotation in 1959, posting a 10-10 record after 21 starts. He would record 11 consecutive double-digit win seasons, relying on a sharp slider and fastball. He never walked more than 83 batters in a season.

Pappas became the standout of the Baltimore staff and started the 1962 All-Star Game. In nine seasons with Baltimore, Pappas never had a losing record. In December of 1965, Pappas was traded to the Cincinnati Reds. He struggled in his first season in the National League, posting a 4.29 ERA, the worst of his career. Yet he managed a winning record at 12-11.

In 1967, Pappas led a burgeoning Cincy staff that included Gary Nolan, Jim Maloney, Sammy Ellis, and Mel Queen. Pappas won a team-high 16 games. But Pappas got off to a slow start in 1968, and the Reds sent him to Atlanta in a six-player trade.

Following the 1966 season, Pappas and veteran Reds pitcher Joe Nuxhall exchanged words through the media. Nuxhall claimed that Pappas was giving less than 100 percent to the club. Nuxhall had to take Pappas's starts twice during the '66 season because Pappas was suffering from "migraines." Nuxhall believed the migraines were simply a case of nerves.

"I've been around baseball long enough to know when a player isn't giving a full effort," Nuxhall said.

Pappas later criticized the Reds organization when they refused to cancel a game the day of Senator Robert F. Kennedy's funeral in 1968. The Reds soon dealt him to the Braves.

Pappas won 10 of 18 decisions for the Braves and had a sizzling 2.37 ERA. But in 1969, Pappas suffered minor injuries that sidelined him briefly in May and June, and then was lost for most of July. The result was a 6-10 record with a 3.62 ERA in 24 starts. Despite his struggles, Atlanta won the NL West title.

In the playoffs, Pappas was used in relief in Game 2 and allowed three earned runs less than three innings, as the Mets swept the series. It was Pappas's only postseason appearance.

The Braves gave up on Pappas after just three starts in 1970, when the right-hander was rocked for a 6.06 ERA and six home runs, including some relief appearances. But Pappas was convinced he could still be a major league starter, and after he was traded to the Cubs on June 23 for cash, he got the chance to prove it. With the Cubs, Pappas went 7-2 in the friendly confines of Wrigley Field with a 2.36 ERA. He finished his first stint as a Cub with a 10-8 mark and a 2.68 ERA. In 1971 and 1972, Pappas enjoyed a resurgence, winning 17 games each season and continuing his winning ways in Wrigley Field. In 1973, he was 9-4 with a 2.25 ERA in Wrigley.

The 1972 season was the best of Pappas's career. He matched his career high with 17 wins, reached the 3,000-inning plateau, pitched a no-hitter, and won his 200th career game.

In 1973, at the age of 33, Pappas struggled to a 7-12 record with a 4.28 ERA. He finished the year with a sore arm, making his last major league start on September 18, at Wrigley against the Phillies in the first game of a doubleheader. He left the game leading 2-1, but the bullpen failed him and his career was over with 209 wins—two more than the man who had scouted and signed him, Hal Newhouser.

In 1998, as Mark McGwire and Sammy Sosa sped past Roger Maris's single-season home run record, Pappas admitted he had grooved a pitch to Maris for his 59th home run in 1961.

Pappas said he threw nothing but fastballs to Maris on September 20, 1961, after telling the Yankee slugger he would do so. "I would do it all over again," said Pappas, who was upset that commissioner Ford Frick was planning to place an asterisk next to the new home run mark should Maris surpass Babe Ruth's mark of 60.

Controversy and personal tragedy would follow Pappas after his playing career.

Pappas' wife went to run errands near their home in Wheaton, Illinois, and disappeared on September 11, 1982.

Pappas started to worry after a few hours had passed. After a few days went by, authorities became involved in a search for Mrs. Pappas.

Speculation arose that she may have been kidnapped. Then Pappas himself was viewed as a suspect briefly. But he voluntarily passed a lie detector test.

Years later, there were no signs of her body, car, clothes or identification. Pappas consulted psychics, searched sanitariums and shelters, and even asked the media for assistance.

Finally in 1987, five years after her disappearance, the car Mrs. Pappas was driving was found in a shallow pond in Wheaton, only four blocks from their home. The pond was hidden from easy view, about 30 yards from the road, behind the Wheaton Fire Department building. The car was located when workers drained the pond to work on the shoreline.

Where Have You Gone?

RYNE SANDBERG

Ryne Sandberg, who gained enshrinement in the Baseball Hall of Fame in 2005, is considered one of the best second basemen to ever play the game.

Following his retirement as a player, Sandberg publicly expressed his desire to become manager of the Cubs, and he demonstrated his willingness to work in the minor leagues to gain experience. Such humility for a Hall of Fame player is rare, and Sandberg experienced some success as a minor league manager. He was named Pacific Coast League Manager of the Year after the 2010 season with the Triple-A Iowa Cubs.

But the organization passed over him each time the big-league job became available, including in 2011 when new Cubs president Theo Epstein decided to go with Dale Sveum as manager. At that point, Sandberg decided to accept a position as manager of the Philadelphia Phillies' Triple-A team. In 2012 he became the third base coach and infield instructor for the Phillies' big-league club.

Sandberg grew up in Spokane, Washington, starring in football and basketball and baseball in high school. Because Spokane has no major league team, Sandberg used to watch the Triple A Spokane Indians play. Bill Buckner, who would later become a teammate of Sandberg with the Cubs, played for Spokane when Sandberg was a youngster.

Otto Greule/Getty Images

23 · RYNE SANDBERG · 2B
Years with Cubs: 1982-1997

Ten-time All-Star • 1984 NL MVP • Nine-time NL Gold Glove Award • Led NL with 40 HR in 1990 • Led NL in runs scored three times • Had 100 RBI in 1990 and 1991 • Hit .300 in five seasons • Batted .385 in postseason career with 1 HR and 6 RBI during 1984 and 1989 NLCS • Totaled 282 HR and 1,061 RBI with Cubs

Ryne got his first name after his parents watched former Yankees pitcher Ryne Duren perform in a game against the Twins in Minneapolis. An older brother, Del, was named after former big league outfielder Del Ennis.

"As a youngster, one of the highlights of the whole year was the entire family taking off during the summer for Thomas Lake," Sandberg said following his National League MVP season of 1984. "We'd go to the same campsite and see the same people every year for two weeks. Fishing, swimming, hiking and just relaxing. For me, that was the big event of the year.

"When I was about nine or 10, my main hobby was catching frogs at the lake. And every year I was sure I had caught the same one. We never marked it, but it seemed like it was always in the same place. We named it Tooly. Tooly the Toad. I'd catch him and keep him a day, then let him go. It took some strategy to catch the frogs. You had to sneak up on them and jump them quick. It was more fun catching the frogs than actually having them. So we'd let 'em go. We even caught fish bare-handed like that.

"Sometimes," Sandberg said then, "I miss those days."

Sandberg, who played for the Cubs from 1981-1994 and again 1996-1997, was acquired in a trade from the Phillies in January of 1982, as a bit of a throw-in. He wound up playing for the Cubs for 16 season. Sandberg won the 1984 National League Most Valuable Player Award, batting .314 with 200 hits, 114 runs, 36 doubles, 19 homers, 19 triples, and 84 RBIs while batting second. Defensively, Sandberg won nine Gold Gloves.

Veteran shortstop Larry Bowa came to the Cubs with Sandberg in the trade that sent Ivan DeJesus to the Phillies. Former Philadelphia manager Dallas Green, the new Cubs' general manager, used his inside information to acquire Sandberg.

A 10-time All-Star, Sandberg stunned Cubs fans when he retired following the 1994 season for personal reasons. But he returned two years later and broke Joe Morgan's record for most homers by a second baseman.

Sandberg hit 277 homers as a second baseman, including 40 homers in 1990. Sandberg is also one of the few players to have both a 40-homer and 50-steal season in his career. In 1990, he played in his 123rd straight game at second without committing an error, then a major league record.

When asked what aspects of the game he missed the most during his brief retirement following the '94 season, Sandberg responded:

"I think I missed being at Wrigley Field, being in front of the fans and really being a part of the team and having fun. That's what I am going back for. I am looking forward to it. I was a baseball player, I am still a baseball player. I don't think it really left me.

"This [return] has been in the makings for a couple of weeks now. I started my workouts. But now that everything is set, I am really psyched up about it. I have had a lot of support. Not only in Chicago, but everywhere. People have asked if I was coming back. It was just really after the season ended that it dawned on me that that was what I wanted to do and that everything was in place as far as I was concerned.

"Taking a year and a half off, I think I appreciate how good the players have it. And they should be enjoying what they are doing and having fun with it. I think that [time off] was good for me. To be a fan of the game, which I will always be, and to go to the ballpark and really sit back and enjoy it...yeah, I think players sometimes get caught up in maybe putting too much pressure on themselves. Or not liking coming to the ballpark everyday. Well, I have a different sense of that now."

Like most former Cubs, Sandberg could not escape the Cubs' postseason hex. His Cubs teams lost in the playoffs in 1984 and 1989. But he did bat .385 with seven extra-base hits in 10 playoff games.

Bump Wills played second base for the Cubs in Sandberg's first season in Chicago. In 1983, Wills left to play in Japan, third baseman Ron Cey was acquired from the Dodgers. Sandberg switched from third to second.

On June 23, 1984, Sandberg enjoyed his most memorable game, driving in seven runs and winning the game for the Cubs, 12-11, over the Cardinals with consecutive home runs off relief ace Bruce Sutter in the ninth and 10th innings. St. Louis manager Whitey Herzog said: "One day I think he was one of the best players in the National League. The next day, I think he's one of the best players I've ever seen." Herzog also referred to Sandberg that day as "Baby Ruth."

SCOTT SANDERSON

A lanky right-hander who pitched 19 years in the big leagues, Scott Sanderson spent six of those seasons with the Cubs, from 1984-89.

Sanderson, who amassed 163 wins and a 3.84 career earned run average, has since worked as a player agent. One of his clients was young pitcher Josh Beckett of the Florida Marlins, who starred during the 2003 National League Championship Series against the Cubs at Wrigley Field.

"I have been working as an agent since the day I stopped playing ball—1997," said Sanderson in 2004. "We are based in Lake Forest, Illinois, and our group is called Moye Sports Associates. I love serving today's ballplayers and trying to continue to bring integrity to the game of baseball. We have a good number of players performing in the major leagues. Just solid players, not only with what they bring to the game on the field, but off the field, as well. Josh Beckett pitches for the Marlins, of course, and it's a learning time for Josh. My partner and I started representing Josh right out of high school."

Sanderson did not hesitate when asked to recall the most exciting time of his 19-year playing career.

"It is kind of a bittersweet memory, but the 1984 season was by far my greatest memory. And when we [former Cub players] see each other, we still say, 'How did we lose to San Diego?' Because we absolutely feel

Brace Photo

21 · SCOTT SANDERSON · P
Years with Cubs: 1984-89

Posted 8-5 record with 3.14 ERA in 1984 • Won 11 games in 1989 •
Totaled 42 wins and appeared in 160 games with Cubs

like we could have gone into Detroit and won the World Series," said Sanderson.

"And we know what it would have meant to this city. There is a little part of us that makes us feel like we kind of let the city down. But it was still a great year for us. I hope the [Cubs] guys this year will take over where we left off here."

Most observers point to the ground ball that went through the legs of Durham in the sixth inning of that 6-3 loss to the Padres in Game 5. But there were other key plays in that series, including the Game 4 start by Sanderson.

"In the fourth game, we had four or five leads, and San Diego kept coming back," said former Cubs manager Jim Frey. "Steve Garvey came up three times and got hits and got them back in the game. And then he hit a home run to beat Lee Smith, and to beat us. Actually, I probably think about the fourth game as much as I do the fifth game. But most fans or sportswriters don't. As a manager, there were so many things that happened in that fourth game. I mean, we could have just blown them out in that fourth game. They are not flashbacks that I have; they are nightmares."

In 1985, Sanderson was one of five Cubs starting pitchers to spend time on the disabled list. He went on the DL in August after partially tearing the medial collateral ligament in his right knee.

"In '85 there was nothing but injuries for everybody," recalled Durham. "I know that we had a chance to continue what we were doing in '84 but our starting five [pitchers] went down and we lost some other players.

Smith, formerly the all-time saves leader in major league baseball, also recalled the injury nightmare of '85 that afflicted Sanderson and other Cubs players.

"Jeff Reardon [then of Montreal] beat me out for the Rolaids Relief Award on the last day of the 1985 season," said Smith. "In 1985, I pitched hurt for the Cubs and I was two points behind Reardon. We had 11 games to play and all I needed was one save so that Jeff couldn't beat me out for that award. Well, the Cubs benched me and I didn't play. We won something like eight out of 11 games and I didn't pitch because I had a $100,000 bonus in my contract for the Rolaids award. That is the only thing that I could say that I regret. If I had known what I know now, I would have said: 'Hey, keep the stinkin' money, I want to win the Rolaids Relief Award,' because I never won the Rolaids Relief Award with the Cubbies. Bruce Sutter had done that for the Cubs in 1981 or '82.

"But it wasn't just me that they benched for contract bonus reasons. They did it to Steve Trout and Davey Lopes. A lot of guys needed only one inning or two at-bats."

Born July 22, 1956, in Dearborn, Michigan, the six-foot, five-inch, 210-pound Sanderson is married to the former Cathleen Cavanaugh. He graduated from Glenbrook North High School in north suburban Chicago. He was named All-State in baseball his junior and senior seasons.

Sanderson was selected by Kansas City in the 11th round of the 1974 amateur draft, but opted to attend Vanderbilt University, where he majored in business finance and history.

In the June, 1977, amateur draft, Sanderson was selected in the third round by the Montreal Expos and this time signed. He had a 9-2 record and 1.41 earned run average in the Venezuelan Winter League following his rookie season with the Class A West Palm Beach club of the Florida State League. Sanderson also had a pair of wins in the Caribbean World Series.

He earned his first major league victory in San Diego on September 2, 1978. Sanderson enjoyed his best season with Montreal in 1980 when he went 16-11 with a 3.11 earned run average. He completed seven games, including three shutouts. In 1983, Sanderson was 6-7. He tore ligaments in his right thumb in a base-running accident against the Cubs in Wrigley Field on July 4 and went on the disabled list.

After six seasons with Montreal, Sanderson was traded to the Cubs in a three-team deal that also involved San Diego on December 7, 1983. The Cubs shipped out first baseman Carmelo Martinez, left-handed pitcher Craig Lefferts and third baseman Fritz Connally.

Sanderson later pitched for the Yankees, A's, Giants, Angels and White Sox during his career.

Where Have You Gone?

RON SANTO

One of the most beloved members of the Chicago Cubs family was Ron Santo, who passed away on December 3, 2010, at the age of 70.

Santo died of complications from bladder cancer.

Immediately following Santo's passing, Cubs chairman Tom Ricketts released this statement: "My siblings and I first knew Ron Santo as fans, listening to him in the broadcast booth. We knew him for his passion, his loyalty, his great personal courage and his tremendous sense of humor. It was our great honor to get to know him personally in our first year as owners. Ronnie will forever be the heart and soul of Cubs fans."

Santo's long-standing pursuit of Hall of Fame recognition was realized posthumously in 2011 when a new Golden Era committee elected the former third baseman for enshrinement in Cooperstown, N.Y., in the summer of 2011. Santo had been up for the Hall of Fame on 19 previous occasions. He first appeared on the Veterans Committee ballot in 2003.

Vicki Santo delivered an emotional Hall of Fame induction speech on behalf of her late husband at Cooperstown, N.Y., in 2011.

Brace Photo

10 · RON SANTO · 3B
Years with Cubs: 1960-1973

Nine-time All-Star • Five-time NL Gold Glove Award • Hit .312 with 30 HR and 114 RBI in 1964 • Had career-high 33 HR in 1965 • Scored 107 runs in 1967 • Totaled 337 HR and 1,290 RBI with Cubs

She thanked the other members of that year's Hall of Fame class: former Reds shortstop Barry Larkin, veteran baseball writer Bob Elliott and broadcast legend Tim McCarver. She also acknowledged the Golden Era Committee that at long last voted Santo into the Hall of Fame. She also thanked his former Cubs teammates Ernie Banks, Billy Williams and Fergie Jenkins.

Vicki Santo's speech was received warmly as many current and past representatives from the Cubs organization made their way to the ceremony to celebrate the life and career of a beloved family member.

"Ron Santo was born to play baseball," she told the audience. "He said his ability to play baseball was a God-given gift, that playing the game was easy, that it was only the diabetes that made the game hard."

Many of Santo's former teammates attended his funeral in Chicago and later reminisced about their playing days with him.

"It all started back in 1959 when we were together (in the minor leagues) in San Antonio, Texas," said Hall of Fame outfielder Billy Williams. "I guess the friendship developed at that time. We had all of those good times in Chicago. And to know him, to be around him, to have conversations with him...not only am I going to miss him, but the people of Chicago will miss him. They need a third baseman up there [in heaven]. So he might go up there and play third base a little bit."

Hall of Fame infielder Ernie Banks, as well as Williams and Santo, now have statues of their likeness outside of Wrigley Field.

"He was just a wonderful person, a really remarkable human being. We are going to miss him a lot," Banks said.

Former Cubs second baseman Glenn Beckert talked about Santo's courage in the face of his lifelong battle with diabetes and accompanying maladies.

"He didn't want to show anybody he was going through severe pain, and the doctor probably told him he was totally terminal," Beckert said. "He's probably up there laughing about all this. And I predict that if the Cubs win the World Series....there he is up there...he finally got one."

Santo hit 342 career home runs and won five Gold Gloves as a third baseman. He played all but one year of his career with the Cubs. His final season was with the Chicago White Sox. He hit 30 homers and batted .300 four times each in his career.

In 1966 Santo hit in 28 straight games. He set a major league record in 1967 with 393 assists at third base. And on May 31, 1966, Santo set a National League record by playing in his 364th straight game at third base. That streak would eventually reach 390. He collected his 2,000th hit on August 26, 1972, at Wrigley Field off the Giants' Ron Bryant. It was a three-run homer that also represented the 1,200th run of his career.

Santo's successes and tribulations were chronicled in a popular documentary entitled *This Old Cub*. His son, Jeff Santo, directed the film that premiered in 2004.

"I had been there with my dad through all of his surgeries. Seeing what happened to him by losing that second leg...my mom said it would be so inspirational to do a documentary on him," said Jeff Santo.

Ron Santo's initial response was guarded regarding his son's idea of creating a documentary centering on his second leg amputation and subsequent rehabilitation.

"At first he was a little apprehensive," said Jeff. "He didn't want a film crew coming around and getting in the way of everybody. But I just felt this film would touch so many people. That's when my dad realized there was a purpose in mind for this film. After that, so many people came on board to help us with this project.

"I said to him, 'This wasn't going to be about a son doing a piece on his father. It's a filmmaker doing a piece on a man.' It was tough at times because there are some scenes where I am filming him with one hand and helping him up with the other hand. You never see me in the film, but a couple of times you see my hand in front of the camera."

Born February 25, 1940, in Seattle, Ronald Edward Santo was signed as an amateur free agent by the Cubs before the 1959 season. Santo was the second former Little League ballplayer to make it to the major leagues. Pitcher Joey Jay was the first. He made his major league debut June 26, 1960.

In his autobiography, *For Love of Ivy*, Santo wrote: "When I was six, my father left home. We lived in an ethnic, middle-class neighborhood called Garlic Gulch, and he was a bartender. He'd come home at three a.m., and you could cut the tension with a knife. He was a wonderful Italian man when he was sober, but sadly, he had a drinking problem that made him vicious, which is how he was at three a.m. My mother, who was Swedish, would be furious, and they'd fight. I'd scramble out of bed to keep him from hitting her, but I was just a kid...and he would beat her.

"They divorced when I was seven. My father had visitation rights to see me and my sister, Natalie, every two or three weeks. We'd wait for him on a corner, and he'd pick us up. One day, he just didn't show up. I didn't see him again for 12 years...

"Sports saved me. The nuns at the school were pretty good athletes—no Babe Ruths, but good enough. And we had a coach named

Vito. Between school and Little League, I was spending a lot of time learning about competitive athletics. I was playing soccer, baseball and football, and to be honest, I actually liked football the best."

Santo and a core of talented players were entrenched in the Cubs lineup for the next decade. Players such as future Hall of Famers Ernie Banks, Billy Williams and Ferguson Jenkins. Many believe Santo deserves to be similarly enshrined. But the fact that this crew failed to win a pennant or World Series championship has not helped Santo's cause to become the fourth member of those teams to be so recognized.

On September 3, 1963, Santo tied an ignominious NL record by committing three errors in one inning against the Giants in a 16-3 Cubs loss.

Santo's best season statistically was 1964 when he hit .312, clubbed 33 doubles, 13 triples and 30 home runs. He drove in 114 runs, walked 86 times and won a Gold Glove. His stats were better than NL Most Valuable Player Ken Boyer, but the St. Louis third baseman helped his Cardinals win the pennant.

Santo led NL third basemen in putouts seven times, assists seven times and double plays four times.

Banks played two years at shortstop next to Santo and eight years at first base. Don Kessinger took over the shortstop role in 1965 and played there for 11 seasons. Glenn Beckert became the starting second baseman in 1965 and stayed there through 1973. Dick Bertell was the Cubs' starting catcher for the first four seasons of Santo's career. In 1966 Randy Hundley became the starting catcher for eight seasons. Williams was starting in the outfield every year from 1961 to 1973.

The manager of those Cubs teams was Leo Durocher, who had favored a set lineup when he led the Dodgers and Giants in the 1940s and 1950s. Banks played at least 150 games 12 times in his career. Santo had a streak of 390 consecutive games played at one time and appeared in at least 160 games seven times. Kessinger played at least 150 games eight times and missed just 43 games from 1968 to 1975. Williams set the NL record for most consecutive games played (1,117).

In December, 1973, the Cubs wanted to trade Santo to the Angels for two young pitchers, but Santo refused because he had played in the league at least 10 years and at least five years with one team. He became the first player to invoke his privilege under the so-called "Ten and Five" rule.

Less than a week later, the Cubs traded Santo to the White Sox for a player to be named later, Steve Stone, Ken Frailing and Steve Swisher. The White Sox later sent the Cubs Jim Kremmel to complete the trade.

A fierce competitor, Santo had his share of run-ins with teammates, opponents, media and managers during his playing career. He would jump up and click his heels after each Cubs win, irritating many opposing players.

In the heat of the division race in 1969, Santo criticized Cubs centerfielder Don Young for making two costly misplays. He apologized the next day, but was booed by fans at Wrigley Field.

Over the years, Santo donated time and money to the Juvenile Diabetes Research Foundation.

LEE SMITH

Eight is enough.

Or was it?

Lee Smith donned eight different baseball caps during his remarkable 18-year major league career. Even though he spent the beginning of his tenure with the Cubs, the game's all-time saves leader already has decided which cap he will wear if and when he is inducted into the Hall of Fame.

"As of right now it would definitely be a St. Louis Cardinals cap," said Smith in 2004. "I had more fond memories and I won the Rolaids Relief Award a couple of times there. I always would consider myself a Cardinal."

The game's most imposing reliever cut his teeth (and his fastball) toiling for the Cubs in the 1980s, amassing 180 of his record-setting 478 saves. Smith walked away from the game because of spotty use by former Montreal Expos manager Felipe Alou. Smith returned home to Castor, Louisana, but he had made it known his then 39-year-old body still had plenty of baseball left in it.

"I talked to the guy [Alou] several times," said Smith. "I went 15 and 16 days without pitching. I went to ask what his wish was and he said he

Brace Photo

47 · LEE SMITH · P
Years with Cubs: 1980-87

Two-time All-Star • Led NL with 29 saves in 1983 • Had career-high nine wins in 1984 and 1986 • Saved 36 games in 1987 • Struck out 112 in 97.7 IP while totaled seven wins and 33 saves in 1985 • Had one save in 1984 NLCS • Recorded 180 saves with Cubs

wanted to keep me around just in case this kid he had in the bullpen got in trouble. I said: "Who's going to get me out of a jam then?"

"I was pitching every two and a half weeks. That was the major reason I retired, because I wasn't getting to play. It wasn't because I didn't want to play. I wasn't getting an opportunity to play.

"I was throwing 92, 93 miles an hour. But every three weeks...? Throughout my career, I have always wanted to pitch two or three times a week. And I was pitching twice a month. I have three kids and I hadn't been home with them that much since I have been playing ball. If I am not going to play, I might as well come home with my family."

Montreal vice president and general manager Jim Beattie said: "I would like to thank Lee for his contribution on and off the field and his years of experience was a great help for our 1997 club."

Less than a month later, Smith was talking about returning to the game.

"I don't have to be the closer. I just want to play. But I don't want to sit around and play every two or three weeks. We had played 90 games in Montreal and I had played in 25. And the rest of the games, I didn't even warm up like I was going to go into the damn games."

Smith had appeared in 1,016 games, the third highest total in history, when he decided to defect from Canada.

"I have 400 and some saves if anybody gives a darn. But my personal goal was that I wanted to break Hoyt Wilhelm's record for the most games pitched in as a reliever," he said. "Getting 500 saves doesn't matter to me as much as the longevity and the consistency thing."

Smith's Cub memories include both highs and lows.

"The 1984 year was awesome," said Smith of that division champion summer. "I have fond memories, and that was the one year that I probably had the most ailments. I had a pulled rib cage. But in the end I can still remember the game in Pittsburgh when Rick Sutcliffe clinched it in 1984.

"In fact, when I went back to Montreal [in '97] to get my stuff, I shared a cab from the hotel to the airport with 'Sut,' because he was broadcasting for the San Diego Padres. We talked about the good old days and he asked me if I would consider coaching if I didn't play any more.

"I told him I wouldn't mind coaching with the Giants, so I could coach for their minor league team in Shreveport, Louisana, and be close to home," said Smith. "If I had to coach I wouldn't want to coach on the major league level because you still have to be away from your family as much as a player."

Smith went from the Cubs to Boston. Then he was traded to St. Louis to the New York Yankees to Baltimore to the Angels to Cincinnati to the Expos.

"The weird thing about my career is that I never played at the same place twice. I have some awesome memories of the years with the Cubs, but the thing about it is we never won anything. I got 30 saves every year, but we never won anything, except for that one [1984] year."

Besides the 1984 season, Smith reflects on other Cub highlights.

"Being the winning pitcher in the All-Star Game in 1987 in Oakland was probably one of my fondest memories with the Cubs," said Smith. "I didn't have to worry about injuries, and I felt healthy."

"The Good Lord kept a good eye on me because I never had any arm troubles," said Smith. "I never missed a game because of my arm. I had a couple of times when my back was stiff and stuff like that, but that was about it."

The list of managers Smith toiled for includes varying personalities. His favorite manager?

"It would have to be Joe Torre," said Smith. "Joe Torre liked the veteran players and he didn't babysit players and he didn't put on airs. If you came to the ballpark and you are late, I don't give a damn if you are a rookie or a 20-year vet, he didn't pull punches because of who you were. If your behind is late, you are late and you are going to get fined. It didn't matter to him who you were. The rules went for everybody, and you don't find many guys like that.

"I didn't look at Joe as the manager the way I looked at others that I had. He was one of the guys, but you respected him as a manager because he wasn't two-faced."

Smith pitched for Torre in St. Louis.

"Torre would say: 'Hey, Smitty, how do you feel? Well, if you're all right I am going to put you in the game tonight.' He would come up to you and ask you how you feel every day. A lot of managers just send the pitching coach over to ask you. Joe Torre wanted to know himself. And I respected that."

Cub fans' most haunting memory of Smith was the home run he gave up to Steve Garvey in Game 4 of the 1984 playoffs in San Diego.

"I had a pulled groin and my rib cage muscle was messed up. Everybody talks about how Steve Garvey hit that home run off of me. But, hell, I had an ace bandage from my armpit to my ankle," he said. "There aren't too many guys who would have gone out there. But the weird thing about it is that that is the thing everybody remembers about

me. But there aren't a whole lot of dudes who would have gone out there
like that.

"I tried to forget about it as soon as possible, because I don't linger
on things," said Smith of the tough playoff loss. "I don't regret the pitches I threw. I would try them again. Garvey is human; he can hit it or miss
it. But it just was that the whole year wasn't good for me because of all
the injuries. And that really hurts me to think about career-wise, because
I didn't have to go out there. But I went out there for the team. There
are very few team players any more.

"Nowadays, if a guys gets a hangnail he goes on the disabled list.
There aren't too many guys who will go out there for the team as much
as we did then. And now, because the teams won't do too much for the
players, the loyalty has been shot to hell."

Smith says his stint with the Cubs was fraught with unfulfilled
dreams.

The Cubs had several future Hall of Famers on their teams in the
1980s, but very few winning ball clubs.

"Andre Dawson won the MVP and Sutcliffe came in with the Cy
Young and we had five hitters set records [for 20 or more homers in a
season]. And then we ended up in the stinkin gutter. Our starting pitching was pretty sad," said Smith.

Smith lapped the field when it comes to saves leaders. But he feels
does not get the respect or notoriety he deserves.

"Nowadays, guys stick their chest out if they pitch one-third of an
inning to get a save," said Smith.

"I have never heard of my numbers used in a positive sense in the
past few years," said Smith in 2004. "I don't know why it is. Some people think it is racial or something. I don't know what it is. I hope the
country still would not be that naive. But how many guys who have the
numbers that I have would have been battling for a nonroster spot on the
Montreal Expos?

"You hear about Randy Myers and Todd Worrell and Dennis
Eckersley. Eckersley is three years older than me and you didn't hear anything about those guys being up there in age.

"I could see that if I had projected a bad image or something, where
I was beating the wife or doing drugs. But the only thing I have done
with the game, I thought, was positive. I try to promote the game of
baseball in a positive sense. What the hell did I ever do to the game but
play ball, sign autographs and try to be nice to everybody?

"Maybe I have been too nice. Maybe I need to strap the hell out of
somebody."

Former Cubs manager Jim Frey traded Smith to Boston when he became general manager.

"He waited three years after I asked him to be traded," said Smith. "I can remember to this day what I said to Shawon Dunston. We were talking about the players on the team who were supposed to be the untouchables. It was supposed to be me and Ryne Sandberg and Shawon and Bobby Dernier and Sutcliffe. And I told Shawon: 'The first sorry sucker to be traded is going to be me. Because I had a good year and I am not making that much money.' I was a prime candidate to get rid of."

Smith was peddled for pitchers Calvin Schiraldi and Al Nipper, neither of whom panned out.

"Ever since then, teams thought there was something wrong with me because of what they traded for me," said Smith. "Ever since they traded for Schiraldi and Nipper, everybody thought there must be something wrong with me for them to trade me for those two guys. Frey had told me: 'Smitty, I will trade you, but I won't take just anything for you.' And then he took the first two sorry guys they offered him."

But Smith was not bitter about being traded from the Cubs.

"The only thing that ticked me off was that it took so long," he said. "I wanted to get traded from the Cubs after 1985 because we had gotten rid of so many guys. I didn't know I was going to last this long. I wanted to get somewhere where I thought I could win something. When they traded me to Boston, we went to the playoffs in 1988 and '89."

Many fans and media members found it difficult to understand Smith when he was with the Cubs, but he was often engaging and always a laugh a minute in the clubhouse.

And Smith had several favorites from the Cubs organization.

"I liked Sutcliffe. And I liked the whole Wrigley Field ground crew. And I remember Bob Serils and Jay Blunk and guys like that from the front office. But I hung out with the guys from the ground crew a lot."

"Ryno was one of my favorites on the team. Ryno, Keith Moreland, Jody Davis, and of course Leon Durham and Sarge [Gary Matthews]." And Smith fondly remembers listening to Harry Caray during the 1980s.

"The only guy I ran into close to Harry Caray was a guy in Anaheim by the name of Bob Starr," said Smith. "Harry really liked me. Harry talked good about me after I came back to play the Cubs. Harry Caray and Vin Scully and Bob Starr...I liked those guys."

Smith was spending plenty of time fishing and relaxing in Louisiana weeks after announcing his retirement.

"My boys [Lee Jr. and Dimitri] had me out there every day, it seems, throwing out a hook," said Smith, who also has a daughter, Nikita.

TIM STODDARD

A hulking, six-foot, seven-inch, 250-pound right-hander with a menacing-looking mustache and beard, Tim Stoddard spent one memorable season of his long career with the Chicago Cubs.

Stoddard was a rare athlete who earned World Series and NCAA basketball championship rings.

He pitched in the big leagues from 1975-88 with the Chicago White Sox, Baltimore Orioles, San Diego Padres and New York Yankees, as well as the Cubs.

Used as a reliever, Stoddard had a 41-35 career record with a 3.95 earned run average, 582 strikeouts and 76 saves in 485 games. He played in the 1979 World Series with the Orioles and was the winning pitcher in Game 4. He also was a member of the 1983 world champion Orioles and the 1984 National League East champion Cubs.

In college, he started at forward for North Carolina State's 1974 NCAA basketball champions.

"We won in 1974, beating Marquette in the semis and UCLA in the finals," said Stoddard, now an assistant baseball coach at Northwestern University in Evanston, Illinois.

"Obviously the big thing was stopping UCLA's reign. They had won eight or nine national titles. So that made that win special. I played with

Brace Photo

49 · TIM STODDARD · P
Year with Cubs: 1984

**Won 10 games and made 58 appearances with seven saves in 1984 •
Pitched 92 innings and had 3.82 ERA • Made two appearances in
1984 NLCS**

great players: David Thompson, who is in the Basketball Hall of Fame now, Tom Burleson and Monte Towe. And Norm Sloan became one of the winningest coaches in his career. I met a lot of great people and a lot of great friends.

"I had thought about [playing in the NBA]. There were a lot of options. But I had signed to play baseball before the ['74] basketball draft," said Stoddard. "The White Sox had drafted me that winter, so they had the rights to me. They put me right on the roster and helped cut off a lot of options. But in the long haul it worked out really good for me."

Stoddard was sent packing by the White Sox after two minor league seasons.

"I got released in the spring after the White Sox made the Goose Gossage for Terry Forster trade," said Stoddard. "Then it seemed like they picked up three million pitchers. I had not even played Class A ball and they were talking about how I might even go play in A ball. I had been expecting to go to Triple A. After I met with the Sox and looked at all the numbers and everything involved, they let me go. By the time I got back to the hotel, there were a lot of calls from other teams."

For the first time in his career, Stoddard began to have a few doubts about his athletic future.

"My oldest daughter was just born and you are trying to get your life settled," said Stoddard. "You think you are going to be playing for a little while. Then all of a sudden that happened. It was kind of a shock. But by the time I got back to the hotel, Kansas City and Baltimore had heard about what had happened. So that made me feel better, knowing I was still wanted."

With Baltimore in 1979, Stoddard posted a 1.71 earned run average in 29 appearances for the American League champions. He had an RBI single in the World Series against the Pirates, the first player ever to drive in a World Series run in his very first major league at-bat.

Stoddard said he holds no grudges against the White Sox organization.

"I see [former White Sox] general manager Roland Hemond all the time. I love and respect the man," said Stoddard in 2004. "There is nobody better in baseball than that guy. We sit and laugh now every time we talk. He said: 'It was not only one of the hardest things I ever did; it was one of the dumbest things I ever did.'

"But the way it worked out, I consider myself fortunate. To be able to play a long time and do things athletes can, you have got to be lucky.

Nobody owes me anything. I owe people for giving me an opportunity to basically play a game my whole life."

Stoddard credits an adjustment he made while in the minors for prolonging his career.

"The biggest thing was when I went into the bullpen when I was in the minors," he said. "Baseball, for a lot of my career, was a secondary sport. I probably never sat there and threw as hard as I could because I was trying to go long distances in a game as a starter.

"Once I went in the bullpen and found out I only had to pitch an inning, I could go out there and throw as hard as I wanted. I ended up picking up three or four miles an hour on the fastball. That ended up being a turning point for me. I had four pitches, but I was basically a two-pitch pitcher—a fastball and a slider. As the years went by, you learn a two-seamer and a four-seamer and do whatever you could to get by."

In 1980 Stoddard led the Orioles with 26 saves. From 1981-83, he shared the Orioles closer role with left-hander Tippy Martinez. But his ERA ballooned to 6.09, and he was traded twice before the 1984 season, first to Oakland and then to the Cubs.

"After leaving the Orioles, where we were winning and competing all the time, coming over to the Cubs at the very end of spring training, the first thought was kind of, 'How is this going to be?'" said Stoddard, who won a career-high 10 games in 1984 and recorded seven saves.

"I was kind of a sixth-, seventh-, eighth-inning guy and Lee Smith was the closer," said Stoddard. "So I was getting into a lot of games that were close and then Smitty would come in and close the door.

"My dad was a huge Cubs fan. So that was real nice for me. Then when I walked into camp and I saw some of the guys we had there, I said, 'Shoot, this isn't a bad ball club at all.' Obviously, throughout that year, [general manager] Dallas Green made some big trades and got some very key components that put us over the top. It ended up being a great year.

"On a personal note, it was the only year I won in double digits. It was my first year in the National League. Coming here, after growing up in the Chicago area, it made everything kind of special. My dad died that winter of cancer. The fact that he got to see pretty much all the games made it a little bit extra special, going as far as we could. I am kind of disappointed that we didn't go further, but those things made (1984) really special to me."

Nonetheless, Stoddard signed a three-year, $1.5 million free agent contract with the San Diego Padres on January 8, 1985.

"I wouldn't have minded staying with the Cubs. But the bad part was that I was a free agent along with Rick Sutcliffe and Dennis

Eckersley and Steve Trout and a couple of other guys. By the time they got to me on the pecking order, there wasn't any money left to help keep me with the Cubs," said Stoddard in 2004.

"Overall, my experience with the Cubs was great. They treat me great now. I go to Cubs Conventions all the time. If I want tickets any time, they get me tickets for family and friends. For me only playing there a year, they have treated me very, very nicely."

On June 18, 1986, Stoddard hit a solo home run in the third inning off the Giants' Mike LaCoss. It was his first major league home run and it came in his last at-bat. He appeared in another 128 games, but never went to the plate.

Stoddard was traded to the Yankees for pticher Ed Whitson in July, 1986. He was used mainly as a setup man for Dave Righetti. Stoddard, who never started a game in 12 major league seasons, was released in August of 1988 with a 6.38 ERA.

Stoddard credits his late father, his siblings and the tough surroundings of the blue-collar steel mill community in East Chicago for preparing him for life. He was a member of East Chicago Washington High School's Indiana State championship team (29-0) in 1971.

"Obviously, growing up in the Northwest Region of Indiana, basketball was *the* sport," said Stoddard. "I played football and baseball, as well as basketball. I don't know if it was the fact I was the number three brother in the whole group, but whatever sport you were playing at the time was your favorite sport. I kind of learned to approach it that way.

"I think being from that area, and as competitive as it was, that kind of helped me down the line as far as realizing that whatever sport that you are playing, you play it as hard as you can. Just for the love of the game."

Stoddard played his high school baseball under longtime coach Jake Arzemenia.

"We had a pretty good high school team. I wouldn't say we were great," said Stoddard. "We would get into the high school tournament, but we wouldn't get real far. We would get through the region area. We had a couple of real good guys on the team, but never enough to get over the hump, it seemed like.

"Jake Arzemenia was a guy who really made it fun to play. We played under the lights in high school at Block Stadium. It was great back then. There were semipro tournaments there all the time. Since we played a lot of night games, it was a fun, special thing for a high school situation.

"I also started playing American Legion ball when I was 15. I had two older brothers and a younger sister. We played whatever sport was going on. And my dad helped with all the Little League stuff. We played Biddy Basketball and Pop Warner football. If nothing else, they kept us busy just to keep us out of trouble more than anything else. And it wasn't hard to get in trouble around there in those days. My dad was a man of few words. But when he said something, he really meant it. He would say, 'If you are going to play and do it, then give it everything you've got. And play as hard as you can.'

"For me, East Chicago, Indiana, was a great place to grow up. You learn to deal with people of every color or race. Basically, my high school was 10 percent white at the time. So it let you learn about diversity and all the different races, dealing with people and judging people for who they were individually—not caring what religion or nationality they were.

"And it wasn't always the safest area, so you learned to be street smart and learn about people pretty well."

Former White Sox infielder Sammy Esposito, a native of East Chicago, Indiana, was the assistant basketball coach and head baseball coach at North Carolina State when Stoddard was sifting through his college scholarship choices.

"Norm Sloan [the N.C. State basketball coach] was from Indiana and he recruited our state a lot," said Stoddard. "And with Sam Esposito having a part in both sports, it made it an easier decision and easier transition walking from the basketball court and going to the baseball field.

"Plus, back then, there weren't a whole lot of restrictions on how many [college baseball] games you could play. Some colleges in the South played as many as 100 games a season."

These days, Stoddard concentrates on grooming young college baseball talent at Northwestern. In September of 2003, Stoddard was inducted into the Chicagoland Sports Hall of Fame.

"Paul Stevens [head coach of the Wildcats] and I had played against each other in college summer ball. He asked if I was interested in coming to Northwestern to coach. I have always enjoyed working with kids," Stoddard said in 2004.

"This situation kind of let me watch my family grow up. If you go back into pro ball, you don't necessarily get that chance again. It has worked out pretty good here. The pitchers have had some success. We had two of them drafted this year—one in the third round [J.A. Happ by the Phillies] and one in the 17th round [Dan Konecny by the Tigers].

"Since I have been here, there has been a pitcher drafted pretty much every year except last year. In that sense it is kind of rewarding for me. We can compete with anybody."

Northwestern claimed its first Big Ten earned run average title in 1995 with a 3.08 ERA in conference games with Stoddard's tutelage. In addition, nine of his pitchers were selected in the MLB free agent draft in previous years—Brad Niedermaier (Twins) and Brian Cummins (Tigers) in 1995, Chad Schroeder (Tigers) in 1996, Josh Levey (Cardinals) in 1997, John Seaman (Cubs) in 1998, Phil Rosengren (Indians) in 1999, Dan Padgett (Giants) in 2000, Michael Nall (Phillies) in 2001, and Gabe Ribas (San Diego) in 2002. Also in 2002, Zach Schara was signed as a free agent by the Texas Rangers.

Stoddard, 60, has three daughters: Laura, Anne, and Ellen.

STEVE STONE

A former starting pitcher with the San Francisco Giants, Chicago Cubs and Chicago White Sox, and a Cy Young Award winner with the Baltimore Orioles, Steve Stone debuted as the analyst on WGN-TV's broadcasts of Cubs games in 1983.

He spent his first fifteen years in the booth alongside the late Hall of Fame broadcaster Harry Caray.

"Harry just loved baseball," Stone recalled. "He used to tell me all the time that he would retire if the Cubs ever won the World Series. I said, 'No, you wouldn't, because you have nothing to retire to. If the Cubs won the World Series, that would be great and you would just want them to win it the next year.' But seeing what has happened to these Cubs fans on a daily basis is something I think would make Harry very happy."

Stone was paired with Chip Caray in broadcasting Cubs telecasts for three seasons on WGN, WCIU and Fox Sports Net Chicago from 1998-2000 before leaving WGN-TV to work as a competition consultant. He returned to the booth with Carary in 2003.

Since Sept. 13, 2008, Stone has been handling Chicago White Sox television color commentary with play-by-play voice Ken Harrelson.

Brace Photo

30 · STEVE STONE · P
Years with Cubs: 1974-76

Went 12-8 and had 3.95 ERA in 214.2 IP in 1975 • Won eight games in 1974 • Won 23 games in 88 appearances and 70 starts with Cubs

Stone also continues to make regular appearances on Comcast SportsNet Chicago, WGN television, and WSCR-AM 670.

A native of Cleveland, Stone began his baseball career while at Kent State University. After graduating from Kent State, he started his 14-year professional baseball career with the San Francisco Giants organization, breaking into the major leagues in 1971.

In 1973, Stone signed with the White Sox. The following year he remained in Chicago, but was traded to the Cubs. He continued his playing career at Wrigley Field through the 1976 season, before returning to the White Sox in 1977 as a free agent. Comiskey Park once again remained his home for the following two seasons.

Then in 1979, as a free agent, Stone signed with the Baltimore Orioles and developed into one of the best pitchers in the American League, helping them become a World Series contender.

In 1980 with Baltimore, he won the American League Cy Young Award after finishing the year with a 25-7 record. His career record was 107-93.

Plagued with elbow trouble during the 1981 season, Stone retired from baseball on June 2, 1982. Following a season on ABC's *Monday Night Baseball*, Stone joined WGN-TV in 1983.

On August 19, 2002, after a two-year absence due to health reasons, Stone returned to the Chicago Cubs television booth for the 2003 season. WGN-TV announced he would work a full schedule of Cubs games alongside Chip Caray for all WGN-TV, WCIU, and Fox Sports Net Chicago broadcasts during the 2003 season.

"This is a very happy day for me," Stone said then. "I'm thrilled to be teamed with Chip again and I want to thank WGN and the Cubs organization for bringing me back.

"I think a couple of years off puts everything into perspective," said Stone. "I don't think anyone can realize how much fun it is to come to the ballpark on a daily basis. We are fortunate enough to make a living at something we love. Sometimes you take that for granted. Coming back feels like an old shoe that you put on, and it is really comfortable."

"It's real hard to make rational decisions when you are just not feeling very well," he said. "In hindsight, I would have asked for a leave of absence as opposed to saying I just didn't want to broadcast any more. Because I was feeling so poorly, I made that decision. I think that at about the middle of the year that I was gone, I started to regret it. Because I did get healthy and I realized how much I missed it."

The Cubs won 67 games in 2002 and 88 games when Stone returned to the broadcast booth. Asked if had taken time to wonder what would have happened if he had not come back to experience the 2003 Cubs' season firsthand, he replied:

"It has been wonderful to experience. But I don't think you can ever deal with 'ifs' and 'buts' and 'what ifs.' I did come back here for this year. I wasn't here last year for 67 wins. I watched a whole lot of them. But it is much easier to call a game when a team is capable of winning 88 games instead of a team that is capable of winning 67."

Over the past two decades, Stone has worked with Harry Caray, Milo Hamilton, Dwayne Staats, Thom Brennaman, Wayne Larrivee and Chip Caray.

"When Harry had his stroke [in 1987], I had the pleasure of working with 34 different celebrities," said Stone. "People like Bill Murray, Ronald Reagan..."

Stone seemed to fit in so comfortably with Harry Caray on Cubs broadcasts for 15 years, trading barbs and keeping up a daily repartee. Then Stone made the transition to working with Caray's grandson in the booth.

"As an analyst in the booth, all you can ask for is enough room from the play-by-play man to get in and get out and make your point," said Stone. "Chip and I worked three years together [1998-2000] and we were very comfortable from the first time we broadcast with one another in Florida. Nothing really changed. To watch Chip mature and turn into a great broadcaster is going to be very interesting to me because I was the guy Harry allowed in the booth."

Born July 14, 1947, Stone enjoyed career highs with nine complete games and 250.2 innings pitched during his Cy Young Award-winning season of 1980. He started 37 games en route to his 25-7 record and 3.23 earned run average. Elbow problems allowed him to finish the following season at just 4-7 before retiring. Before 1980, Stone's career high in victories was 15 in 1977 with the White Sox.

Stone had to serve as Harry Caray's straight man in many unintentionally comical on-air episodes.

"I think the one thing that stands out about Harry Caray is the fact that every day he comes to the park, it is like Christmas for him," Stone said when Caray celebrated his 50th year in the broadcast booth. "It really doesn't matter where the team is; he just loves baseball.

"It is very easy for people to point out what Harry isn't. They say he is not poetic like Vin Scully. He is not lyrical like Bob Costas. He is not a wordsmith like some of the other greats. But he is the single greatest salesman of the game of baseball that ever lived. I believe the game will suffer a huge loss when Harry decides to stop broadcasting, for one reason or another.

"There are a lot of people who clamor for his resignation. They say he should step down or he should do this or do that. But you are looking at a dinosaur. There will never be another Harry Caray. So what if he mangles a few words and gets some names wrong. In the end, what difference does it make? The object of baseball is for everyone to enjoy themselves. In the seventh inning, no matter where we go, everybody stands up and looks to the booth, looks to Harry. He is a people magnet. He is a unique character that the game will never see the likes of again.

"I think people should overlook a malaprop or two or a mispronunciation of one of the names, and just say: 'Look, let's enjoy him while he is here.' Because I really believe that when he is gone, there will be a lot of people who miss Harry."

Stone had to bite his tongue on occasion, overlooking an obvious mistake made by Caray on the air.

"I do that all the time, but I realize that eventually, we will get it right up there," he said. "Most of the time, it really doesn't matter that much. Occasionally, I would correct him, but not often. The fans who are watching the game, they know who is coming up to bat. They can see the name on his back. They can certainly recognize Andres Galarraga by now. They can recognize Barry Bonds when he calls him 'Bobby' Bonds. People know that Bobby Bonds was a coach and Barry Bonds is a hitter. It would take a pretty obtuse baseball fan not to recognize the difference between those two guys."

These days, Stone is the broadcaster who is becoming a breed apart, enlightening baseball fans with his keen insight and experience.

Where Have You Gone?

RICK SUTCLIFFE

R ick Sutcliffe was a Cy Young Award winner and an All-Star. Yet the current ESPN baseball analyst admitted in 2004 the game is much easier from the broadcast booth.

"You have to keep reminding yourself that it is not easy," said Sutcliffe, who pitched for the Cubs, Dodgers, Indians, Orioles and Cardinals. He finished his career with a 171-139 record and 4.08 earned run average.

"I think the best thing that I do is coach a high school team in Kansas City, also. You go back and watch those guys play and you remember how difficult it is to do the things that these guys at the big league level can do. Plus, I still rove around to do the minor league [scouting] thing [for the Padres]. I appreciate what they are able to do out there."

The big redhead was NL Rookie of the Year with the Dodgers before going 16-1 with the Indians and Cubs in 1984.

"For me, my best memory was in Chicago at the old Comiskey Park in 1983," he said. "Even though you know you are an All-Star and you have done some good things, just to see your name on that locker alongside some of the others is just something you will never forget."

Brace Photo

40 · RICK SUTCLIFFE · P
Years with Cubs: 1984-91

Two-time All-Star • Won 1984 NL Cy Young • Led NL with 18 wins in 1987 • Went 16-1 with 2.69 ERA in 1984 • Won 18 games in 1987 and 16 in 1989 • Went 1-1 in three career postseason starts and batted .500 with one HR in postseason career • Totaled 82 wins in 190 starts with Cubs

Richard Lee Sutcliffe was born June 21, 1956, in Independence, Missouri. The six-foot, seven-inch, 240-pound right-hander became a Cub on June 13, 1984, when his contract was purchased from the Cleveland Indians along with catcher Ron Hassey and reliever George Frazier. In return, the Cubs dealt outfielders Joe Carter and Mel Hall. On June 13, 1984, the Indians also received pitchers Don Schulze and Darryl Banks. And on April 1, the Cubs also received outfielder Pookie Bernstine to satisfy a player-to-be-named requirement of the deal.

Sutcliffe became only the third pitcher in Cubs history to win the Cy Young Award in 1984 when he compiled a 2.69 earned run average after being acquired from Cleveland. He recorded 155 strikeouts and seven complete games.

Sutcliffe graduated from Van Horn High School in Independence, Missouri, where he earned All-State honors in baseball, football and basketball. He was a high school All-American in baseball and football. He played for the Babe Ruth League national champions, and in high school recorded a 20-4 pitching record as a senior.

He was the No. 1 selection of the Dodgers in the June 1974 amateur free agent draft. After being named the outstanding rookie in Dodgers spring training camp in 1977, Sutcliffe enjoyed his finest minor league season in 1978 at Triple A Albuquerque of the Pacific Coast League. He had a 13-6 record and 4.45 ERA in 30 games.

In 1979, Sutcliffe made the Dodgers' roster, initially as a reliever. After nine appearances out of the bullpen, he subbed for starter Burt Hooton against Philadelphia on May 3. Sutcliffe went the distance in beating the Phillies 5-2. He remained in the rotation the rest of the way and led the staff with 17 wins. Sutcliffe was named National League Rookie of the Year as he set a franchise record for wins by a rookie.

One of Sutcliffe's most memorable performances with the Cubs came in September of 1984 against the Pirates in old Three Rivers Stadium.

The Cubs captured the National League East Division title behind Sutcliffe's masterful two-hitter.

Sutcliffe struck out nine and walked none as the Cubs defeated the Pirates 4-1 for the organization's first title since 1945.

The burden of a franchise and a proud city were lifted as the Cubs scratched the 39-year itch that had represented the team's scarlet letter.

"This ball club has suffered for 39 years, and that's long enough," said Cubs manager Jim Frey, popping the cork on a bottle of champagne that seemed to represent the pent-up emotions of a deprived organization.

"Everybody said this club had a monkey on its back. Now the monkey's off."

At the conclusion of the regular season, the Cubs would face the West Division champion San Diego Padres in a best-of-five League Championship Series beginning October 2, 1984, at Wrigley Field.

But Sutcliffe's division-clinching performance was a climax to a Cinderella story that defied all odds. A team that had finished fifth the previous season, a team that had lost 11 straight preseason games in the spring of '84 and finished with the worst exhibition record in all of baseball was suddenly ruling its division.

"We're league busters," shouted Cubs first baseman Leon Durham, dousing ace reliever Lee Smith with champagne.

"The most I've ever seen is one bottle of champagne at one time," said Smith with a laugh. "These guys are frying my natural. It'll cost me $75 to get my hair done again."

"I'm going to savor the hell out of this moment," said right fielder Keith Moreland.

"We've tried to show the fans in Chicago that we love them. Those 40,000 fans are our 10th man. I feel like we can't lose at Wrigley Field with them behind us. I'm looking straight at this thing. I'm looking at us winning the World Series."

"This was a special moment for me and a special moment for my wife," said former Cubs general manager Dallas Green on that memorable night. "It's been a tough three years for us and she's hung in there."

"This is just a wonderful feeling," added Stanton R. Cook, former president and chief executive officer of Tribune Co. "To see this team progress ... we saw how they looked in spring training ... is just an amazing experience."

The Cubs played with the same looseness that magical night in Pittsburgh that was their signature throughout the season.

Frey said he had noticed a difference in the team's personality before the previous Sunday's doubleheader sweep of the Cardinals that ended a season-high five-game losing streak and reduced their magic number to one.

"We spent an uncomfortable week after all the hullabaloo in Chicago," said Frey. "I recognized in the clubhouse before Sunday's games that the players were talking a little differently. It was more, 'We have to go out and win it ourselves,' instead of waiting for someone else to help us."

Sutcliffe, with his 14th straight triumph, earned his 20th victory of the season overall, becoming only the fourth pitcher in major league history to accomplish the feat while crossing leagues. He improved his record to 16-1 with the Cubs, after going 4-5 with Cleveland, making him the first 20-game winner in the majors in 1984.

Left-hander Larry McWilliams, who beat the Cubs 11-6 the previous week in Chicago, took the loss for the Pirates.

Gary Matthews, who raised his league-leading number of game-winning runs batted in to 19, gave the Cubs a 1-0 lead in the first inning. It was his third straight game-winning RBI.

A crowd of only 5,472 paid was on hand for the historic event at Three Rivers Stadium.

When Green and other Tribune Co. executives—Cook, Andy McKenna and John Madigan—emerged from their box seats behind the Cubs' dugout to go to the team's clubhouse in the bottom of the eighth, the Cub fans on hand gave them a standing ovation.

"That's when it finally began to sink in to me that this thing was really going to happen for us and the city of Chicago," said Cook.

The Cubs would go on to win the first two games of the best-of-five NLCS series at Wrigley Field against San Diego. Sutcliffe would even smack a home run in the 11-0 first-game shellacking.

Needing to win just once in San Diego, the Cubs dropped all three. They had a 3-0 lead with Sutcliffe on the mound when the Padres rallied to win 6-3 in Game 5.

Many Cubs fans have second-guessed Frey's decision to stick with Sutcliffe after he got into trouble in the late innings, instead of going with a more rested pitcher such as left-hander Steve Trout, who was 13-7 in 1984.

"I don't second-guess anything that I did with the use of the pitchers," Frey said in 2004 "I would do the same thing. But in the fourth game, there were some situations with a pinch hitter I might have changed. In Game 5, I can understand why someone would sit back and say that I left Rick Sutcliffe in there too long. But there are two things you have to remember. Number one, Sutcliffe had not lost a game since June. And I wouldn't say that Steve Trout was the most dependable guy that we had ever run into.

"I mean, we got a good year out of Trout, and he hung around the big leagues a long time. But I think he won more for me than he did anybody else. So bringing him in was no guarantee. Same thing happened this past [2003] playoff season in Boston. Their manager had Pedro Martinez struggling on the mound. I had Sutcliffe. Martinez is obviously one of the best pitchers in the last several years. Do you go to a lesser guy? Even though I am separated from the game all these years, these things still pop up."

Where Have You Gone?

STEVE TROUT

A key starter on a Cubs' division championship team, Steve Trout had his most productive major league season in 1984 when he went 13-7.

Trout also pitched for the White Sox, Yankees and Mariners. But his fondest memories are with the Cubs.

"I still hear people say that the Cubs have had some outstanding teams, but the '84 team was the most fun," said Trout in 2004. "That was the year that things really started to change at Wrigley Field. People started coming out to the ballpark and it was about having fun. It was a fun year for me."

A couple other pitchers who were teammates of Trout with the Cubs—Jamie Moyer and Greg Maddux—continue to pitch well in the big leagues. Moyer won 21 games at the age of 40 for the Mariners in 2003. And Maddux had won at least 15 games every year over a 16-year period—a major league record—entering 2004 for his second tour of duty with the Cubs.

"We used to make a lot of jokes with Jamie that he used to be able to do it with smoke and mirrors," said Trout. "And Maddux has been able to do the same thing with hard work and being a student of the

Brace Photo

34 · STEVE TROUT · P
Years with Cubs: 1983-1987

Was 13-7 with 3.41 ERA in 1984 • Won nine games and had 3.39 ERA
in 1985 • Had 10 wins in 1983 • Was 1-0 in two games in 1984 NLCS •
Totaled 43 wins in 138 appearances with Cubs

game. They were smart not to change their approach to pitching. And Greg is a good athlete, as well."

Trout saw early on that Maddux and Moyer would be able to succeed with grit and guile.

"Greg was smart because he wasn't hanging around with me," Trout said with a laugh. "That was very important. He went out to the best restaurants. But early on, I saw Greg as a student of the game. He didn't overwhelm you with his stuff. And he wasn't oversized [six feet, 170 pounds then]; he wasn't lanky or anything. There was almost a question as to whether he was going to make it or not. But he was someone who was going to make himself better. That's the key thing. He was hitting his spots and he knew that was all he had to do. To me, that was the intelligence that he carried. He was a guy who wasn't going to beat himself. Almost like Jamie Moyer."

Known as an eccentric, fun-loving personality during his playing days, Trout seems to have settled down and matured since his retirement from the game.

He once missed a scheduled start against the Reds when he said he fell off a bike near his home. Meanwhile, Pete Rose was chasing Ty Cobb's all-time hits record, so young Reggie Patterson had to start the game for the Cubs and gave up Rose's record-tying hit at Wrigley Field.

Trout has dabbled in various ventures since hanging up the cleats, including being a player agent, writing, coaching, and engaging in entrepreneurial ventures.

Born July 30, 1957, in Detroit, Trout is the son of Paul "Dizzy" Trout, who pitched for Detroit in the 1945 World Series against the Cubs. Paul Trout, who died February 28, 1972, in Chicago at the age of 56 when Steve was 14, had a lifetime record of 170-161 in 15 big-league seasons.

Steve finished his career with a record of 88-92 and a 4.18 earned run average.

Steve Russell Trout grew up in South Holland, Illinois and graduated from Thornwood High School in 1976. His high school teammates nicknamed him "Rainbow." Trout was selected by the White Sox in the first round (eighth player overall) in the '76 June draft. He made his major league debut on July 1, 1978.

After going 37-40 with the White Sox, he was traded to the Cubs on January 26, 1983, with pitcher Warren Brusstar in exchange for pitchers Dick Tidrow and Randy Martz and infielders Scott Fletcher and Pat Tabler on January 25, 1983.

In 1984 Trout led the Cubs staff in innings pitched (190) and starts (31). He won six straight starts from May 16 to July 3. On May 30, 1984, Trout had a no-hitter for seven and two-thirds innings at Atlanta and wound up being the winner in a 6-2 triumph. He tossed a 3-0 shutout against the Mets on July 29 in New York. It was his first shutout since 1980. He also blanked the Braves 5-0 on Aug. 26.

Trout continued to help the Cubs win the National League East title with his impressive 3.41 earned run average. In the best-of-five NLCS against the San Diego Padres, Trout went eight and two-thirds innings in Game 2 of the Cubs' 4-2 victory that gave them what appeared to be a commanding two games to none advantage.

But the Cubs would go on to lose the next three games in San Diego for a heartbreaking ending to an otherwise fairy tale season.

Some observers felt former Cubs manager Jim Frey should have gone to Trout earlier out of the bullpen in Game 5 when starter Rick Sutcliffe was beginning to tire in the sixth inning of that loss.

Sutcliffe was the National League Cy Young Award winner in 1984 and had gone 16-1 with the Cubs after being traded from the Cleveland Indians early in the season.

In 1985, Trout was off to a 6-1 start when he injured the ulnar nerve in his left arm. His record was 8-4 with a 2.82 earned run average when he was placed on the disabled list on July 23. He returned to the active roster on Aug. 24 and finished the season with a 9-7 record and a career-low 3.39 ERA.

While Trout had a rocky relationship with Frey, he did work closely with his pitching coach, Billy Connors. Trout realizes now how important it is to be on the same page with the coaching staff.

"The Cubs players today seem to want to play well in front of their coaches—[hitting coach] Gary Matthews, [pitching coach] Larry Rothschild and [bench coach] Dick Pole. They want to impress them. To me, that's really important when you want to impress your coaching staff. The players respect them that much," said Trout.

In 1986, Trout was used as both a starter and reliever by the Cubs as Gene Michael took over the managerial duties on June 13 of that season. Trout was 4-7 with a 5.14 ERA in 25 starts in '86. As a reliever he was an effective 1-0 with a 2.38 ERA in 22 2/3 innings. Trout allowed six home runs in 1986—five of them to Montreal batters. He did not allow a home run to a left-handed hitter all season.

Known for his devastating sinker, Trout induced the opposition to ground into 19 double plays. And 54 percent of his outs were on ground balls. He recorded at least 10 ground ball outs in 10 of his 25 starts.

But elbow problems continued to plague him. Trout was traded to the Yankees in 1987 in exchange for pitcher Bob Tewksbury and two minor league pitchers. But Trout was incredibly wild and had an 0-4 record in the Big Apple. He was sent to Seattle on December 22, 1987, along with outfielder Henry Cotto for pitchers Lee Guetterman and Clay Parker and minor leaguer Wade Taylor. Trout finished 4-7 with a hefty 7.83 ERA in 1988.

It was in Seattle that Trout was paid his highest salary—$990,000— in 1988. But he was released by the Mariners on June 12, 1989, with a 4-3 record and 6.60 ERA.

BILLY WILLIAMS

Small wonder Billy Leo Williams became known as one of the greatest two-strike hitters in baseball. He had two strikes against him, it seems, growing up in Whistler, Alabama.

"Whistler is a place that is filled with pride and I believe Whistler still cares a great deal about Billy," said Williams's former high school civics teacher, Mrs. Valena McCants, who also served as a surrogate mother to all of the children of Whistler. "When Billy made it to the Hall of Fame, I had to feel that the whole community accomplished something right along with him."

Williams, now an executive advisor for the Cubs, reminisced about his nearly four decades in professional baseball.

"When I was in my prime as a ballplayer, I surely didn't think I would be in baseball when I was 66 years old," said Williams in 2004. "But baseball grabbed me. As a matter of fact, when I first came into the big leagues I said I was going to play 10 years and then I was going to retire. But I have enjoyed the game so much. I have spent about 44 or 45 years in the game of baseball. And I am still enjoying it."

Taking a visit to Williams's hometown just prior to his induction into baseball's Hall of Fame in 1987, there seemed to be very little worth preserving in this impoverished southern outpost near the dock of the

Brace Photo

26 · BILLY WILLIAMS · OF
Years with Cubs: 1959-1974

Six-time All-Star • 1961 NL Rookie of the Year • 1972 NL batting champion with .333 average and led league in slugging percentage • Led NL with 205 hits and 137 runs in 1970 • Hit 42 HR with 129 RBI and .322 average in 1970 • Had 100 RBI in three seasons and hit over .300 in five seasons • Totaled 392 HR and 1,353 RBI with Cubs • Elected to Baseball Hall of Fame

bay—save the beautiful people, the beautiful trees and the beautiful memories.

There were shabby boarded-up shanties, desolate dirt roads and abandoned shelters converted into churches, where the inner strength, faith and purposefulness of the humble congregations belie the frailty of the makeshift structures.

But the confidence of these people today remains sturdy, resounding, unshaken.

There was overwhelming conviction that Sweet-Swingin' Billy Williams, one of their native sons, at long last would be delivered into baseball's Hall of Fame.

The disappointment of Williams's previous failures to reach the hallowed Hall—including the near miss by four votes in 1986—did not discourage his legion of friends in that seaport community or across the nation. The people of Whistler continued to dream the Impossible Dream.

"In 1987, my grade school principal, Mrs. Lilly A. Dixon, passed away," Williams said. "I mentioned her in my Hall of Fame speech. She always talked about the 'good, better, best' idea. My high school coach, Virgil Rhodes, passed away. And the lady who delivered me passed away. She was 93 years old. My father passed away several years ago. He died at 92 years old. He lived a good, long life and he got to see me perform in the major leagues. He enjoyed what I enjoyed."

Williams's birthplace remains a welcome throwback to a simpler life where baseball and family values seem to go hand-in-hand.

Williams beat some astounding odds along with several other major league stars from this greater Mobile, Alabama, area. Four of them are in the Hall of Fame, including the Negro League legend pitcher Satchel Paige. All-time home run leader and Hall of Famer Hank Aaron is from Mobile, along with his late brother, Tommy Aaron, who played briefly in the big leagues. Willie McCovey, the lanky Giants slugger, is a native of Mobile who was inducted in 1986. Former Mets star Cleon Jones was Williams's teammate from Plateau, Alabama, and longtime big-league outfielder Tommy Agee was also a teammate at the once-segregated Mobile County Training School in Whistler. Outfielder Amos Otis and infielders Frank and Milt Bolling are also from that area.

"Henry Aaron, Willie McCovey, Cleon Jones, Tommie Agee, Amos Otis....at one time the New York Mets had three guys in their outfield from Mobile. That's kind of unusual," said Williams. "We are all proud of that. We all went off to play baseball and we wanted to be the best ballplayers up in the big leagues. We proved it over the years with the home runs, the MVP awards, and the Rookie of the Year awards. In fact, Willie McCovey, Tommy Agee and I were all Rookies of the Year.

"A lot of guys from our area got [big-league] contracts, but they didn't want to leave home," said Williams. "My brother signed in 1955, and I guess he inspired me to play baseball. We used to have many conversations about how nice it was. I said: 'That's what I want to do.'"

Becoming a big hit outside of Whistler, Alabama, was no minor feat, however.

"During the time Billy came through [in the late 1950s], the odds of him making it out of this area were just about insurmountable," said Charles T. Rhodes, his former football coach, who passed away recently. "We had no baseball team when Billy was in high school, and the facilities at the school were not good at all. All the black kids had to go to Mobile County Training School, and if he wanted to go to college and play ball, there were few opportunities at that time."

Like the rest of the Mobile County Training School students, Williams was required to wear a white or blue shirt and a black tie every day, even though the parents could barely afford to dress them. Seniors wore red ties to distinguish themselves from the underclassmen. In-school discipline and respect for the teachers were understood.

"I used to step on a student's foot or do whatever I had to do in those days to get them to respond," said Mrs. McCants, who later worked in the president's office at Bishop State Junior College in Mobile. "You can't do that sort of thing any more. But I also would walk home with the students on occasion. That wasn't uncommon. That's the kind of upbringing Billy had."

Williams appreciates that upbringing to this day.

"It was a common practice of all the teachers to kind of see their pupils as their kids," said Williams. "That is how it was."

An opportunistic Williams helped make his breaks along the way to move on from the section of Whistler known as "Baptist Town." He played sandlot baseball in neighborhood clearings such as Prichard Park and Mitchell Field.

With great reverence, Williams recalls the names of Ed Tucker, the owner of an area semipro team; Edward Scott, who later scouted for the Red Sox; and Jessie Thomas, who scouted and signed McCovey for the Giants.

"I've known Billy all of his life, managed him on some sandlot teams," said Thomas, whose brother, "Show Boat" Thomas, played for the New York Cubans of the old Negro League and had a tryout with the old Brooklyn Dodgers the year before Jackie Robinson broke the color line.

"Of all the players out of Mobile, I thought Billy was one of the best," said Thomas. "I feel the Mobile area owes all of those guys a lot. And you will never find a guy more respected than Billy Williams."

Williams eventually was spotted by Cubs scout Buck O'Neil, the same eagle-eyed talent seeker who uncovered Hall of Fame slugger Ernie Banks. Ivy Griffin later signed him to a contract.

While Rhodes used to emphasize the gentlemanly nature of Williams, the late veteran in the field of education once recalled with apparent pride that he paddled Williams as a youngster.

"Did Billy ever tell you I used to paddle him?" Rhodes said with a sinister grin years ago. "Well, yeah, I put the wood on him a couple of times. I don't remember what it was for exactly. But evidently he stepped beyond my rules a couple of times and I laid it on him.

"He thanked me for it later. But Billy was a kid you didn't find in the office all the time. If I had a son—and I've got three daughters—I'd certainly want him to be like Billy."

Many elder residents in Whistler, Alabama, know Williams as "Jessie May's Boy" and Williams has returned periodically to pay his respects. Mrs. Carrie Turner, a former neighbor, once recalled young Billy playing marbles in her yard with the same fierce competitiveness that was his signature in the batter's box.

His mother, the former Jessie May Moseley, passed away in 1977, and his father, a former sandlot ballplayer of some local renown, still called the old Williams residence at 2939 Pyton Street his home until he passed.

"I'm so proud of Billy. I think he should have been put into the Hall of Fame a long time ago, if you ask me," said Frank "Susie" Williams, a retired railroad worker and a right-handed-hitting first baseman whose sweet swing earned him such a sweet nickname as a player. "Billy always did have that nice swing, but I tried to teach him to play third base when he was a kid. He was kind of tall and I thought he'd make a good third baseman. But I guess he did fine in the outfield."

Williams slugged 426 homers, drove in 1,475 runs and hit .290 over 18 seasons (16 with the Cubs).

"I had him practicing every evening with Tommy Aaron and his brother, Henry," Williams's father said after his son's induction.

Williams is one of five children. Older brother Franklin was thought to be the best athlete of the family.

"Billy's mother was a very supportive parent, and I think that's where his strength came from," said Mrs. McCants. "They were a humble, big family. I also taught Billy's wife, Shirley. She was from Plateau. Billy was a couple of years older than Shirley and I would always try to keep them separated when they were in school. He would always come around and I'd tell Shirley, 'You'd better stay away from Billy Williams because he's too old for you.' Well, you can see now how that turned out. They have four lovely daughters now. Billy's a lovely boy, though."

Rhodes, the high school football coach for Williams, Agee and Jones, used to say there was little early physical evidence to predict that Williams would become a professional athlete.

"In terms of his physical attributes, you wouldn't believe he'd achieve what he did," Rhodes said in 1987. "But in terms of tenacity, Billy was a little wiry kid, probably didn't weigh more than 150 pounds soaking wet in high school. But he had good hands and good reflexes, so I put him in the secondary, mostly, even though he was listed as an end. He wasn't what you would call a blue-chipper as a football player. I was surprised he made it to the majors in baseball. Evidently he picked up some strength along the way and made himself into a top athlete.

"The only thing I tried to tell Billy or any of the kids I coached in football along the way was to do the most you can and try to reach your optimum level," said Rhodes. "If that's not good enough, tough."

Williams was the National League Rookie of the Year in 1961, hitting 25 homers and driving in 86 runs in only 146 games while batting .278. His best seasons were in 1970 and 1972, both worthy of league MVP honors. The Reds' Johnny Bench beat him out both years largely because his team was a winner while the Cubs were floundering.

Williams hit .322 with 42 homers, 129 RBIs and 137 runs scored in 1970. In 1972 he won the NL batting title with a .333 average and slugged 37 homers.

Williams had 13 straight seasons of 20 or more homers' and he wound up with a career batting average of .290. Before his induction, he was the only player with more than 400 homers who was not in the Hall of Fame.

As bench coach and hitting coach for the Cubs for several seasons, Williams prided himself on being able to work with players on all facets of the game.

"I would throw batting practice every day. That was my exercise. I enjoy life to the fullest, and I enjoy my grandkids. I have four grandkids (William, Nicolette, Jasmine and Jeran) and they all live right around me," said Williams. "We get to see them every day and we play baseball with them."

Approaching his 66th birthday in 2004 put Williams in a reflective mood, recalling his former teammates and friends.

"Baseball was my life growing up, and it still is my life now. I think about it when I am going home and I think about it when I am home. My wife and I talk about it. It has just been a part of my life."

Williams was surrounded by family, friends and longtime former teammates as a statue of his likeness was unveiled during a ceremony at the corner of Addison and Sheffield, just outside of Wrigley Field in September of 2010.

Former teammates Ernie Banks, Ferguson Jenkins, Glenn Beckert, Randy Hundley and Ron Santo were in attendance as Williams' wife, Shirley, daughters and grandchildren watched the long-awaited depiction of "Sweet-Swinging" Billy Williams.

"I really appreciate you guys being here," Williams said as he stood at the podium in front of hundreds of fans who stood outside the ballpark. "You could see how much fun we had in the '60s. It's a joy to know these individuals. I know that Ernie, Fergie, Beckert, Randy Hundley, Ron Santo have been great teammates. But most of all, they're great friends because we've been together for so long."

Williams thanked new Cubs owner Tom Ricketts and the rest of the Ricketts family, "for making this possible."

The sculpture was commissioned by renowned sculptor Lou Cella of the Rotblatt-Amrany art studio in Highwood. Illinois.

"When you look at his numbers and what he has done...an all-around player...not just a real great hitter, but a good ballplayer, a smart ballplayer and a wonderful guy," Santo said.

"I think the people here knew it was time for Billy," said Tom Ricketts. "He is such a wonderful man. Not only was he a great player, but he has been a classy member of this organization for all of these years. So it just made sense to go ahead [and build a statue for Williams]."

Where Have You Gone?

KERRY WOOD

The fourth overall pick of the 1995 amateur baseball draft, hard-throwing 6-foot, 5-inch Kerry Wood from Irving, Tex., and Grand Prairie High School would become one of the most popular Cubs players of the past two decades.

Of course, Wood, known by adoring Chicago fans as "Kid K," will be revered forever because of his starring role in one of the most memorable performances in franchise history. As a rookie righthander making just his fifth career start on May 6, 1998, Wood struck out a major-league record-tying 20 Houston Astros batters en route to a pulsating one-hit victory at Wrigley Field.

The remarkable feat tied Roger Clemens' big-league mark of 20 strikeouts in a nine-inning game. Wood was named National League Rookie of the Year after finishing with a 13-6 record. He missed the last month of his rookie season with a sore elbow.

While Wood's career began in auspicious and electric fashion, it ended in a more subdued, poignant manner when he was summoned from the bullpen on May 18, 2012 and struck out the only batter he faced- Dayan Viciedo of the Chicago White Sox. Word had circulated before that game that the 35-year-old Wood had planned to announce his retirement. As he was lifted from the game one last time, Wood

AP Photo/Daily Herald, George LeClaire

#43 KERRY WOOD • P
Years with Cubs: 1998-2008, 2011-2012

Went 13-6 and had 3.40 ERA in 166.2 IP in 1998 when he was named National League Rookie of the Year • Struck out 20 batters vs. Houston in 1998 to tie Major League record • Won a career-high 14 games in 2003

received a standing ovation from the Wrigley Field partisans and he was met at the steps of the dugout by his young son, Justin, who gave his dad a memorable hug.

The Cubs celebrated Kerry Wood Appreciation Day on September 23, 2012, at Wrigley Field. He had pitched 12 years for the Cubs and finished with 1,470 strikeouts for Chicago, third-most in club history. Wood appeared in four playoff series. His modest 86-75 career win-loss record does not tell the entire story of what kind of pitching talent and clubhouse leadership Wood possessed. He had a career earned run average of 3.67 and had 1,582 strikeouts, including his years with the Indians (2009-10) and Yankees (2010).

"I am glad to be able to start this journey from here on out," Wood said of his retirement. He also thanked his father for teaching him to play the game "the right way." Teammates stood behind Wood as he spoke to the media from a podium set up at home plate on a very hot day at Wrigley Field. Wood thanked his wife, Sarah, and other family members that also include daughters Charlotte and Katie and son Justin.

Wood talked about how much he appreciated Jim Hendry, Dusty Baker, Oscar Acosta, Larry Rothschild, Lester Strode and others in Cubs management and coaching for their influence on his baseball career and life. Wood also thanked teammates, clubhouse employees and fans. He even thanked the media for their fairness and respect, "even though it wasn't exactly a love affair," he said with a smile. Laura Ricketts, a member of the Cubs ownership family, then presented Wood with a series of gifts from the organization, including a framed picture of his 20-strikeout game.

Hendry and Wood go way back together—all the way back to the beginning of Wood's professional career when Hendry was a scout. Hendry was fired by the Cubs as general manager in 2011 and then was hired as special assistant to Yankees GM Brian Cashman. Wood had signed a one-year, $3 million deal with the Cubs for the 2012 season.

"I'm glad he got to go out the way he did…to go out and throw and finish off with a big out at the time," Hendry said of Wood's dramatic exit. "I'm sure emotionally [retirement] has been weighing on him for awhile. And he always does the right thing for the Cubs. It would have been easy to play it out the rest of the year. Obviously he chose to lessen the burden he felt he was putting on the club."

Unfortunately, Wood endured some 14 stints on the disabled list with a variety of arm, finger and shoulder injuries that impeded his career. He spent two years with the Cleveland Indians and New York Yankees as a reliever, and he was at peace knowing that his days as a starter were over. Coming back to Chicago for the 2011 season made sense from both a family and professional standpoint. His wife grew up in suburban Waukegan, Ill., and the Woods had set up a foundation in Chicago that continues to support charitable causes.

Former Cubs Hall of Fame third baseman and WGN Radio broadcaster Ron Santo was a good friend of Wood, and ironically it was Santo's funeral in December of 2010 that brought Wood back to the Cubs. Sarah made her feelings known to her husband, as well.

"It kind of happened quick," Wood said of his return to the Cubs. "I brought it up to her. She had mentioned it to me here and there. And I said: 'It's not possible, it's not happening. Quit thinking about it.' Then, obviously, we saw everyone at Santo's memorial service, and then at the funeral the next day. We started seeing everybody and she started talking more about it. And, you know… it's just not going to happen. Then I was just thinking, 'Why not? Why couldn't it happen?' This is where I want to be and this is what I want to do. We'll see what happens. Just kind of threw it out there to Jim Hendry, just to see what was out there. And he was honest from the minute one. He said: 'I don't think we're going to be able to do anything,' but he would get back to me. He said, 'I won't get back to you unless we can pull something off.' A few days later we were inking the deal."

Fair or not, Wood and fellow young right-handed phenom Mark Prior shared sagas of unlimited potential that was too often compromised by frequent injuries. Media and fans joked about how many "towel drills" Wood and Prior had to perform throughout their Cubs careers while rehabbing sore shoulders or aching elbows. Wood even missed the entire 1999 season after undergoing Tommy John surgery. Asked how he was able to deal with their shared legacies, Wood said:

"It was pretty simple for me. I had a few years, I had established myself. I had a few years in. So, [Prior] was a great teammate. He had great stuff, obviously. It was unfortunate that he did not have a prolonged career."

Wood couldn't help at times but agonize over the Cubs' close encounter in 2003. Just five outs away from beating the Marlins in Game 6 to capture the NLCS, the Cubs famously faltered behind a suddenly rattled Prior, and a bungled double-play ball by shortstop Alex Gonzalez. Known as the "Bartman Game" because of the fan who famously reached over to catch a foul ball that Cubs leftfielder Moises Alou may or may not have been able to catch, the Cubs franchise seemed to remain cursed.

Still with a chance to send the Cubs to the World Series for the first time since 1945, Wood started Game 7, but could not stop the Marlins. The Cubs and Wood lost that game 9-6, even though Wood hit a home run. It was the first time a pitcher had homered in the NLCS since former Cub Rick Sutcliffe went deep in the 1984 NLCS against the San Diego Padres.

"I think most guys getting toward the end of their career look at that season where they got the closest. I mean, 'What if, what if, what if?'" Wood said.

"It's just kind of the way it goes. If we had been able to pull that off for the city of Chicago, for this organization and for the fans, it would obviously be special to be a part of. You would never forget it because they would never let you forget it. That team would be linked for history. We would be linked for the rest of our lives— all 25 guys. You think of it from that respect. But I don't really think of it from a personal standpoint, just more so along the lines of for the city and the organization."

Wood had signed a one-year deal for $1.5 million in 2011, well below his market value around the league. But the deal was personal for him and his family. Wood said the grass is not always greener on the other side, and he was glad to be back home in Chicago.

Following his retirement, Wood immediately spent time relaxing with his family in Chicago and away from the daily grind of icing his aching shoulder and traveling throughout the country. Speculation quickly grew that Wood would have some sort of role within the Cubs organization in the future.

In the meantime, Kerry and Sarah remain passionate about The Wood Family Foundation (www.woodfamilyfoundation.org), which is a non-profit organization that was established in June 2011. The foundation works to improve the lives of children in and around Chicago by raising funds and awareness for children's charities and the causes they support.

Wood even broke ground on a $5 million baseball field named after him near Lane Tech High School on Chicago's north side on Oct. 11, 2012. Wood, who spent his first three years of high school at MacArthur High School in Irving, Tex., knows the importance of having decent facilities as a young ballplayer.

"It is an honor to be a part of this project that will help keep public school baseball teams local during playoff season," Wood said. "We want this field to benefit student athletes in many ways for years to come."

The Kerry Wood Field project was made possible through contributions from the Chicago Cubs, Chicago Cubs Charities, Wood Family Foundation, City of Chicago, Chicago Park District, Chicago Public Schools and Turner Construction.

Kerry Wood Field was expected to be completed in 2013, at which time it would be owned and operated by the Chicago Park District. The field, which will include seating for 1,100 fans, was intended to be used by Chicago public high schools citywide throughout the high school baseball season during and after school hours. The Park District also expected to use the field for recreational leagues and for use by the general public.

There was an additional Cubs connection to the field being built next to Lane Tech High School. Legendary Cubs outfielder Phil Cavarretta played at Lane Tech before making his Wrigley Field debut on Sept. 25, 1934. Cavarretta was the NL MVP in 1945 and led the Cubs to their last World Series appearance in 1945 when they lost to the Detroit Tigers.

Sarah Wood is happy to have her husband home, joking that he would be called upon to car pool immediately. The couple had talked about his retirement several times previously, but she knew it would be his decision to make, and when the time was right, he would do what was best for him and everyone else concerned.

DON ZIMMER

The uniforms and some of the names around him may have changed. But Don Zimmer has remained a fixture in major league baseball for nearly six decades.

The 82-year-old Tampa Bay Devil Rays coach, a veteran of 56 years in professional baseball, cherishes his memories as manager of the Chicago Cubs. He also played for the Cubs in the early 1960s and served as a third base coach under his lifelong friend, Jim Frey, with the Cubs in the early 1980s.

"I wish I could have stayed [with the Cubs]," said Zimmer. "I loved it. My biggest thrill in baseball—regardless of all the teams I have been with—was in 1989 when we clinched the Eastern Division title in Montreal. That was the biggest thrill I have had in baseball. I have been on a three-time World Series team. They are all great thrills. But in my own heart, the biggest was winning the division title with the Cubs when nobody else ever thought we could win. The guys just played their hearts out. I look back now and try to figure how we won. I just can't believe it. If we wanted a squeeze bunt, they executed. If we wanted a double steal, they executed. The players did everything."

Born January 17, 1931 in Cincinnati, Ohio, Donald William Zimmer donned five different uniforms as a player. He played third base,

Brace Photo

17/4 (MANAGER) · DON ZIMMER · SS
Years with Cubs: 1960-61 (player); 1988-91 (manager)

All-Star in 1961 • Totaled 19 HR and 75 RBI with Cubs • 1989 NL
Manager of the Year • Won 93 games and NL East title in 1989 •
Posted 265-258 record with Cubs.

second base, shortstop and catcher from 1954-65 with the Brooklyn Dodgers, Chicago Cubs, New York Mets, Cincinnati Reds and Washington Senators. He had a career batting average of .235 in 1,095 games, and hit 91 home runs. He later managed the Boston Red Sox, Texas Rangers and Cubs.

"This is my favorite place for me and my wife," Zimmer said of Chicago.

On July 7, 1953, the scrappy five-foot, nine-inch, 170-pound Zimmer was leading the American Association with 23 home runs and 63 runs batted in when he was hit on the head by a pitch from Jim Kirk.

Zimmer was unconscious for nearly two weeks. He lost his ability to speak for six weeks and lost 44 pounds. Doctors inserted what Zimmer describes as four "buttons that looked like tapered corkscrews in a bottle." Zimmer returned to the game in 1954 and was the Brooklyn Dodgers' second baseman in the 1955 World Series. But in 1956, another pitch—this time from Cincinnati's Hal Jeffcoat—fractured Zimmer's cheekbone and ended that season for him.

The determined Zimmer would not be denied. He was the Dodgers' starting shortstop in 1958, achieving career highs of 17 home runs and 60 RBI. In 1959 he lost his job to the speedy Maury Wills as the Dodgers defeated the Chicago White Sox in the World Series. After playing two years with the Cubs, Zimmer became an original New York Met. He finished his playing career in Japan.

The Cubs had acquired Zimmer from the Dodgers on April 8, 1960, in return for infielder John Goryl, outfielder Lee Handley, minor league pitcher Ron Perranoski, and cash. Perranoski would emerge as the top reliever in the National League.

One highlight of Zimmer's playing career with the Cubs occurred on September 18, 1960. Zimmer, Ron Santo and George Altman hit sixth-inning home runs as the Cubs beat the Dodgers 5-2 at Wrigley Field. He batted .258 in 1960 for the Cubs and .252 with 13 homers in 1961.

Zimmer went to the Mets on October 10, 1961, in an expansion draft involving the Houston Colt 45s (now known as the Astros) and the Mets.

Selecting first, Houston took Giants shortstop Eddie Bressoud. Then the Mets took 31-year-old Giants catcher Hobie Landrith. Second choices were infielders Bob Aspromonte for Houston and Elio Chacon for the Mets. Other Houston selections were Bobby Shantz, Ken Johnson, Dick Farrell, and Bob Lillis. New York grabbed Roger Craig, Gil Hodges, Gus Bell, Jay Hook, and Zimmer among others.

CHICAGO CUBS: WHERE HAVE YOU GONE?

On May 6, 1962, the Mets acquired pitcher Vinegar Bend Mizell from the Pirates for first baseman/outfielder Jim Marshall, then sent Zimmer to Cincinnati for pitcher Bob Miller and infielder Cliff Cook.

As the manager of the Cubs in 1989, Zimmer was able to oversee a renaissance of sorts in the Chicago sports world.

The 1989 Cubs were just 13-15 in the month of June, but they finished 17-11 in September and the Cubs won their second NL Eastern Division championship in 1989.

Led by Zimmer, the Cubs enjoyed All-Star seasons from Ryne Sandberg, Andre Dawson, Rick Sutcliffe and with relief pitcher Mitch Williams along with Rookie of the Year performance by outfielder Jerome Walton. The San Francisco Giants defeated the Cubs in the NLCS four games to one.

Always fiercely competitive and loyal, Zimmer jumped to the defense of Frey during spring training of 1984.

The increased media attention at the Cubs' spring training camp focused mainly on the battle for the shortstop position between 22-year-old Shawon Dunston and incumbent 39-year-old veteran Larry Bowa.

During the 2003 ALCS between the Boston Red Sox and New York Yankees, Zimmer did not act his age (72) when he went after Red Sox pitcher Pedro Martinez. Zimmer, then a bench coach with the Yankees, was tossed easily to the ground by Martinez along the first base line as both benches emptied and fans booed. Zimmer was helped from the field and order was finally restored.

The Tampa Bay Rays announced that Zimmer will return as senior adviser in 2013. This will be Zimmer's 10th season with the Rays out of 65 total seasons in professional baseball.